REFLECTIONS

EDL GO Series Book 9

SENIOR EDITOR
Estelle Kleinman

EDITOR
Nancy Carleton

ASSISTANT EDITOR
Diane Bello Peragine

COMPREHENSION CHECK QUESTIONS BY
Nancy Carleton

DESIGNER
Donatien Nicolas

ILLUSTRATORS
Kim Zimmerman
Paul Rátz de Tagyos

Cover photo © Tom Pantages

ISBN 1-55855-204-9

7 8 9 10 EB 05 04 03

CONTENTS

All the Years of Her Life

by Morley Callaghan

They were closing the drugstore, and Alfred Higgins was putting on his coat and getting ready to go home. The little gray-haired man, Sam Carr, who owned the drugstore, looked up and said softly, "Just a moment, Alfred. One moment before you go."

The soft, confident, quiet way in which Sam Carr spoke made Alfred start to button his coat nervously. He felt sure his face was white. Sam Carr usually said "Good night" without looking up. In the six months he had been working in the drugstore, Alfred had never heard his employer speak softly like that. His heart began to beat so loud it was hard for him to get his breath. "What is it, Mr. Carr?" he asked.

"Maybe you'd be good enough to take a few things out of your pockets and leave them here before you go," Sam Carr said.

"What things? What are you talking about?"

"You've got a compact and a lipstick and at least two tubes of toothpaste in your pockets, Alfred."

"What do you mean? Do you think I'm crazy?" Alfred protested. His face got red and he knew he looked fierce with indignation. But Sam Carr only nodded his head a few times, and then Alfred grew very frightened and he didn't know what to say. Slowly he raised his hand and dipped it into his pocket, and with his eyes never meeting Sam Carr's eyes, he took out a blue compact and two tubes of toothpaste and a lipstick, and he laid them one by one on the counter.

"Petty thieving, eh, Alfred?" Sam Carr said. "And maybe you'd be good enough to tell me how long this has been going on."

"This is the first time I ever took anything."

"So now you think you'll tell me a lie, eh? You think I don't know what goes on in my own shop, eh? I tell you you've been doing this pretty steady."

While Sam Carr stroked the side of his face very delicately with the tip of his fingers, Alfred began to feel that familiar terror growing in him that had been in him every time he had got into such trouble.

"I liked you," Sam Carr was saying. "I liked you and would have trusted you, and now look what I've got to do." While Alfred watched with his alert, frightened blue eyes, Sam Carr drummed with his fingers on the counter. "I don't like to call a cop in point-blank," he was saying as he looked very worried. "You're a fool, and maybe I should call your father and tell him you're a fool."

"My father's not at home. He's a printer. He works nights," Alfred said.

"Who's at home?"

"My mother, I guess."

"Then we'll see what she says." Sam Carr went to the phone.

Alfred was not so much ashamed, but there was a deep fright growing in him, and he said proudly, like a strong, full-grown man, "Just a minute. You don't need to draw anybody else in. You don't need to tell her." He wanted to sound like a big guy who could look after himself, yet the old childish hope was in him, the longing that someone at home would come and help him.

"Yeah, that's right, he's in trouble," Mr. Carr was saying. "Yeah, your boy works for me. You'd better come down in a hurry." And when he was finished, Mr.

Carr went over to the door and looked out at the street and watched the people passing in the late summer night. "I'll keep my eye out for a cop" was all he said.

Alfred knew how his mother would come rushing in; she would rush in with her eyes blazing, or maybe she would be crying, and she would push him away when he tried to talk to her, and make him feel her dreadful contempt; yet he longed that she might come before Mr. Carr saw the cop on the beat passing the door.

While they waited—and it seemed a long time—they did not speak, and when at last they heard someone tapping on the closed door, Mr. Carr, turning the latch, said crisply, "Come in, Mrs. Higgins." He looked hard-faced and stern.

Mrs. Higgins must have been going to bed when he telephoned, for her hair was tucked in loosely under her hat, and her hand at her throat held her light coat tight across her chest so her dress would not show. She did not look as Alfred had thought she would look: She smiled, her blue eyes never wavered, and with a calmness and dignity that made them forget that her clothes seemed to have been thrown on her, she put out her hand to Mr. Carr and said politely, "I'm Mrs. Higgins. I'm Alfred's mother."

Mr. Carr was a bit embarrassed by her lack of terror and her simplicity, and he hardly knew what to say to her, so she asked, "Is Alfred in trouble?"

"He is. He's been taking things from the store. I caught him red-handed."

As she listened, Mrs. Higgins looked at Alfred and nodded her head sadly. When Sam Carr had finished, she said gravely, "Is it so, Alfred?"

"Yes."

"Why have you been doing it?"

"I've been spending money, I guess."

"On what?"

"Going around with the guys, I guess," Alfred said.

Mrs. Higgins put out her hand and touched Sam Carr's arm with an understanding gentleness, and speaking as though afraid of disturbing him, she said, "If you would only listen to me before doing anything." Her simple earnestness made her shy. She faltered and looked away, but in a moment she was smiling gravely again, and she said with a kind of patient dignity, "What did you intend to do, Mr. Carr?"

"I was going to get a cop. That's what I ought to do."

"Yes, I suppose so. It's not for me to say, because he's my son. Yet I sometimes think a little good advice is the best thing for a boy when he's at a certain period in his life," she said.

Alfred couldn't understand his mother's quiet manner, for if they had been at home and someone had suggested that he was going to be arrested, he knew she would be in a rage and would cry out against him. Yet now she was standing there with that gentle, pleading smile on her face, saying, "I wonder if you don't think it would be better just to let him come home with me. He looks a big fellow, doesn't he? It takes some of them a long time to get any sense." They both stared at Alfred.

But even while he was turning away uneasily, Alfred was realizing that Mr. Carr had become aware that his mother was really a fine woman; he knew that Sam Carr was puzzled by his mother, as if he had expected her to come in and plead with him tearfully, and instead he was being made to feel a bit ashamed by her vast understanding. While there was only the sound of the mother's soft, assured voice in the store, Mr. Carr began to nod his head encouragingly at her. "Of course, I don't want to be harsh," Mr. Carr was saying. "I'll tell you what I'll do. I'll just fire him and let it go at that. How's that?" He got up and shook hands with Mrs. Higgins, bowing low to her in deep respect.

There was such warmth and gratitude in the way she said, "I'll never forget your kindness," that Mr. Carr began to feel warm and genial himself.

"Sorry we had to meet this way," he said. "But I'm glad I got in touch with you. Just wanted to do the right thing, that's all," he said.

"It's better to meet like this than never, isn't it?" she said. Suddenly they clasped hands as if they liked each other, as if they had known each other a long time. "Good night, sir," she said.

"Good night, Mrs. Higgins. I'm truly sorry," he said.

The mother and son walked along the street together, and the mother was taking a long, firm stride as she looked ahead with her stern face full of worry. Alfred was afraid to speak to her, he was afraid of the silence that was between them, so he only looked ahead too, for the excitement and relief were still pretty strong in him; but in a little while, going along like that in silence made him terribly aware of the strength and the sternness in her; he began to wonder what she was thinking of as she stared ahead so grimly; she seemed to have forgotten that he walked beside her. Finally, he broke the silence and said, "Thank God it turned out like that. I certainly won't get in a jam like that again."

"Be quiet. Don't speak to me. You've disgraced me again and again," she said bitterly.

"That's the last time. That's all I'm saying."

"Have the decency to be quiet," she snapped. They kept on their way, looking straight ahead.

When they were at home and his mother took off her coat, Alfred saw that she was really only half-dressed, and she made him feel afraid again when she said, without even looking at him, "You're a bad lot. God forgive you. It's one thing after another and always has been. Go to bed, why don't you?" When he was going, she said, "I'm going to make myself a cup of tea. Mind, now, not a word about tonight to your father."

While Alfred was undressing in his bedroom, he heard his mother moving around the kitchen. She filled the kettle and put it on the stove. She moved a chair. And as he listened there was no shame in him, just wonder and a

kind of admiration of her strength and calm. He could still see Sam Carr nodding his head encouragingly to her; he could hear her talking simply and earnestly, and as he sat on his bed, he felt a pride in her strength. "She certainly was smooth," he thought. "Gee, I'd like to tell her she sounded swell."

And at last he got up and went along to the kitchen, and when he was at the door, he saw his mother pouring herself a cup of tea. He watched and he didn't move. Her face, as she sat there, was a frightened, broken face utterly unlike the face of the woman who had been so assured a little while ago in the drugstore. When she reached out and lifted the kettle to pour hot water in her cup, her hand trembled and the water splashed on the stove. Leaning back in the chair, she sighed and lifted the cup to her lips, and her lips were groping loosely, as if they would never reach the cup. She swallowed the hot tea eagerly, and then she straightened up in relief, though her hand holding the cup still trembled. She looked very old.

It seemed to Alfred that this was the way it had been every time he had been in trouble before, that this trembling had really been in her as she hurried out half-dressed to the drugstore. Now he felt all that his mother had been thinking of as they walked along the street together a little while ago. He watched his mother, and he never spoke, but at that moment his youth seemed to be over; he knew all the years of her life by the way her hand trembled as she raised the cup to her lips. It seemed to him that this was the first time he had ever looked upon his mother.

Accent on Ability

by Richard B. Lyttle

Henry (Hank) Viscardi was thirty-seven years old when he made the most important decision of his life.

It was 1949, and Viscardi worked in New York City, directing the personnel department in charge of hiring and firing employees for a large and successful company. The $15,000-a-year job provided challenge and a secure future. Viscardi considered himself successful.

But then friends asked him for help, and Henry Viscardi started to have second thoughts about success and what it meant. His friends wanted him to head a newly formed, very experimental organization aimed at finding jobs for the disabled. There would not be much pay, and there would be no security. But the challenge was monumental.

As Viscardi thought about the challenge, his job with the New York company seemed unreal. But the decision did not come easily. He had worked hard for his position, and with a wife and family to support, the high salary and the security of his job could not be taken lightly. Besides, hadn't he fulfilled his obligation to the disabled? He had worked day and night during World War II, training amputees who had lost their legs or arms to use artificial limbs. He had even tackled the tough task of breaking down prejudices among employers against disabled workers.

The new organization was called J.O.B., standing for Just One Break. After being asked to head it, Viscardi

UPI/BETTMANN NEWSPHOTOS

Dr. Henry Viscardi (top left) is shown applauding President Ford after the President announced that the White House Conference on Handicapped Individuals (chaired by Dr. Viscardi) would be held in Dec. 1976.

discussed the offer at length with his wife, Lucile. Later that same evening, they went next door and continued the discussion with Dr. Robert Yanover and his wife, Sunny, both close friends of the Viscardis.

Lucile and the Yanovers told Hank the job sounded exciting, and no one could be better suited for it than he. But the decision had to be his alone.

Hank continued undecided until he received a visit one day in his New York office from a friend, one of the amputees he had helped during the war. The friend made him realize that the symbols of success that surrounded him were not all-important. He could do better things with his life.

As soon as his friend left his office, Hank picked up the telephone and accepted the job. His entire life, from the day he was born, had been a preparation for such work. He knew he had the ability to meet the challenge, and he knew that a good part of that ability was his because he had been born without legs.

Life had not been easy for Hank. For his first seven years, his home was the hospital. Doctors operated again and again to straighten his stumpy limbs, hoping the boy might be able somehow to walk. Eventually, the stumps were fitted with padded boots that looked like upholstered boxing gloves. It was awkward and tiring, but Hank learned to move about the hospital ward without help.

Soon after Hank left the hospital to live at home, he started school. It was difficult to leave the sheltered life he had always known. The first day, he was teased without mercy and promptly nicknamed "Ape Man." His short, jerky stride did suggest an ape. Soon Hank himself decided it was an apt nickname and accepted it with good humor.

Though he learned to adjust to school and made friends easily, he wondered why he had to be different from everyone else. One night, just before bed, he asked his mother about it. His mother, a devout Catholic, explained that it was God's will.

Hank's father died while the boy was still in high school, and it became necessary for him and his oldest sister to help support the family. Hank reported high school sports for *The New York Times* and earned additional money refereeing basketball games.

Meanwhile, Dr. Robert Yanover, who came to Long Island soon after the Viscardis, took an interest in Hank's case. He warned Hank he was in danger of overworking his stumps. For several years, Hank did not heed the warning.

He was more active than many youths his age, and in 1930, when he graduated from high school and entered Fordham University in New York City, he combined his classwork with work in the university treasurer's office. He continued refereeing basketball games to pick up extra money. And, as if that weren't enough, he worked as a busboy in the campus cafeteria. Financial problems forced Hank to leave school and look for full-time work, but eventually he enrolled in night school to study real estate law.

Hank already had strained his stumps beyond the limit. The pain sometimes made it impossible for him to stand. Even binding the stumps in bandages failed to ease his agony. Hank made an appointment with his old friend, Dr. Yanover.

"Your legs have burnt out," the doctor said after an examination. He told the patient bluntly that he would be living in a wheelchair in another six months.

Hank shook his head. Couldn't something be done? he asked.

There was one other chance, just a hope, Dr. Yanover explained. It might be possible to fit Hank with artificial legs.

The idea left Hank stunned. He tried to blank it out of his mind. It was too big a hope. Should he even consider it? Dr. Yanover persuaded Hank that he should. The doctor ordered him to quit work and drop out of night school to give his legs a rest. He would need all the strength he could summon.

The first limb-makers to examine Hank said the request was impossible. With such short stumps, no artificial limbs could be considered.

Hank gave up hope. Dr. Yanover did not. He persuaded Hank to visit George Dorsch, a German limb-maker who worked in a dusty shop hung with arms and legs and hands and feet—all of wood and metal. It seemed to Hank like a wax museum.

Dorsch rudely refused to listen to Dr. Yanover's explanation of Hank's case. It was too much for Hank to hear his friend insulted, but before he could get up to leave, he was placed on an examination table, where Dorsch and his assistants went to work at once taking measurements.

Dorsch, far ahead of his time in the science of limb-making, finally stepped back, smiling. He said, "I think we can do it. We will make the limbs of aluminum."

During the weeks that followed, Hank sometimes faced bewilderment. How tall did he wish to be? Dorsch wanted to know. What size shoe? Hank had never considered such questions. Dorsch shrugged. He decided to give Hank a size eight shoe and make him stand five feet, eight inches tall. Hank, who had been three feet, eight inches tall throughout his adult life, simply gaped at the old German.

Hank kept the project a secret from his family and friends. If the legs did not work, he alone would bear the disappointment.

Finally the day of the first fitting arrived. Dorsch, friendlier by this time, spoke about quality—both in limbs and in the people who wore them. The legs he was lacing on were top quality, Dorsch explained. Hank understood.

Then, after Dorsch found a pair of old trousers to cover the aluminum legs, he lifted Hank erect and half carried him to a corner of the room where there was a metal bar to hold for support. As Hank clung to the bar, Dorsch bounded back across the room and swung out a full-length mirror.

Hank stared. He saw a stranger staring back. And yet, it was no stranger. Hank Viscardi gripped the metal bar tightly and wept without shame. He felt he had been born again, and he was overcome with emotion.

But there was much work to be done, and Dorsch became a stern instructor. Day after day he drilled Hank in the use of the new legs. On his first attempt to walk with two canes, Hank fell to the floor, crying with defeat. Dorsch made him try again. Finally, Hank took his first step, then another and another.

When Hank felt confident enough with the legs to wear them home for the first time, he created a sensation. His family welcomed him with laughter and tears. Hank felt he was walking on air, instead of on aluminum legs.

Dr. Yanover refused a fee and even protested Hank's expressions of deep gratitude. "Tell you what you can do, though," the doctor said. "Someday maybe you'll have the chance to bring new life to another man. If you can help someone else feel the way you do today, that's all I ask."

Soon Hank could walk without his cane, and his sisters taught him to dance. And he began to court a young woman.

But still more changes lay ahead. When the Japanese attacked Pearl Harbor on December 7, 1941, Hank Viscardi decided to get into uniform. He was able to join the Red Cross, which planned to use him as a field officer—not as a hospital worker, as he had wished.

However, just before he was to be sent overseas, high-ranking army officers heard of the Red Cross officer with artificial legs. The Red Cross at last was persuaded to assign Hank Viscardi to Walter Reed General Hospital in Washington, D.C.

Hank was devoted to the work and put in long hours, often helping and encouraging patients well into the evening. But he was bothered by Red Cross and army regulations and was sharply critical of the hospital's old-fashioned artificial limbs.

Viscardi's no-nonsense talk with military representatives resulted in the improvement of the quality of these limbs. And today, the artificial limbs provided by the military are the best available.

Soon after the war, Hank met Lucile Darrocq, a map-maker with the broadcasting company for which he worked. When Hank proposed, Lucile accepted.

They were married on November 16, 1946, and moved into a remodeled garage on Long Island, a garage belonging to Hank's old friend, Dr. Yanover.

By 1949, the Viscardis were well launched on a peaceful, postwar life. They had two daughters, and the family was still growing. Hank's switch to the top personnel job seemed to assure the Viscardis of a comfortable, secure future.

Then came a telephone call from Olin Lehman, member of a prominent New York banking family. Lehman, an amputee interested in rehabilitation, had already described the idea of the Just One Break organization to

Hank. Lehman wanted Hank to head the venture.

The visitor from the past, the amputee Hank had once helped, gave Hank the answer. He left his comfortable position for the daring new job. He has never regretted the move.

And thousands upon thousands who have found work through J.O.B. can be thankful for Henry Viscardi's decision. With faith, hard work, and persistence, Viscardi and the men and women he placed in jobs have demonstrated that the disabled are valuable workers. Many of the old prejudices have been dispelled.

In 1955 Hank established the Human Resources Research and Training Institute. The institute tests the capabilities and potentials of workers and also teaches certain skills necessary for factory and office jobs. The institute benefits more than two hundred trainees annually.

In 1962 Hank launched the Human Resources School. At the start, there were three teachers and fourteen pupils. In eight years, the enrollment grew to nearly two hundred pupils. Of those graduated, more than two-thirds have gone on to colleges or universities.

Through his work, writing, and talks, Viscardi stresses again and again that employees should be considered for their ability, not their disability.

"All of us are physically limited," he once said. "It's just a matter of degree. Many of the disabled have developed other special qualities to offset the extremes of physical makeup."

Henry Viscardi knows about that severe test of suffering. He knows the problems, and when he talks, people listen. For a man who did not attain his full height until the age of twenty-six, Henry Viscardi stands tall indeed.

One Good Time

by Mary Wilkins Freeman

Richard Stone was nearly seventy-five years old when he died; his wife was over sixty; and his daughter Narcissa past middle age.

All the village was scandalized at the shabby attire of the widow and daughter at the funeral, except William Crane.

''William Crane never took his eyes off Narcissa Stone; shouldn't be surprised if he married her in a month or six weeks,'' people said.

William Crane was about Narcissa's age, but he looked older. His gait was shuffling, his hair scanty and gray, and he had that expression of patience which comes from long waiting, both of body and of soul.

William visited after the funeral and looked at Narcissa anxiously with soft, patient eyes. ''How are you gettin' on?'' he asked.

The kitchen was very familiar to him, but tonight it looked strange. For one thing, the armchair to which Richard Stone had been bound for the last fifteen years was vacant and pushed away into a corner. It seemed to William that he could see the crooked, stern old figure in it, and hear again the tap of the stick which he kept always at his side to summon assistance. After his first glance at the dead man's chair, William saw his widow coming forward.

"Oh, William, do you know what we're goin' to do?" she wailed. "We're goin' to take the insurance money and go to New York. I tell Narcissa we hadn't ought to, but she won't listen."

William looked pale and bewildered, and his voice trembled when he spoke. "This ain't true, is it, Narcissa?"

Narcissa's eyes were glowing, her hair tossing in loose waves. She looked as she had when he first courted her. "Yes, it is, William Crane," she cried. "Yes, it is."

She stood and talked with feverish haste. "I'm going to take that money and go with Mother to New York, and you mustn't try to stop me. I know what you've been expecting. I know, now Father's gone, you think there ain't anything to hinder our getting married. I know you ain't counting on that insurance money; it ain't like you."

"The Lord knows it ain't, Narcissa," William broke out with pathetic pride.

"I know that as well as you do. You thought we'd put it in the bank for a rainy day, in case Mother got feeble, and that is all you did think.

"Maybe I'd ought to. I s'pose I had, but I ain't going to. I ain't never done anything my whole life that I thought I ought not to do, but now I'm going to. I've made up my mind. I ain't never had one good time in my whole life, and now I'm going to even if I have to suffer for it afterward.

"I've never had any clothes nor gone anywhere. I don't know anything about the world nor life. I don't know anything but my own old tracks, and—I'm going to get out of them for awhile, whether or no.

"It ain't many men would have waited for me as you've done, when Father wouldn't let me get married as long as he lived. If you think you'd rather marry somebody else, I won't blame you—"

"Maybe you want me to, Narcissa," said William with sad dignity. "If you want to get rid of me, if that's it—"

"That ain't it." She hesitated. She had the usual reserve of a New England village woman about expressions of affection, and had never even told her lover in actual words that she loved him. "My feelings toward you are the same as they have always been, William."

They stood close together for a moment. He stroked back her tumbled hair with clumsy tenderness. "You've had a hard time, Narcissa," he whispered, brokenly. "If you want to go, I ain't going to say anything against it. I ain't going to deny I'm kind of disappointed. I've been living alone so long, and I feel kind of sore sometimes with waitin' but—."

"I shouldn't make you any kind of a wife if I married you now. I tell you, William, I've got to jump my wall, and I've got to have one good time."

William Crane nodded in patient acceptance. "How long do you calculate to be gone?"

"I don't know," she replied. "Fifteen hundred dollars is a good deal of money. I s'pose it'll take us quite a while to spend it, even if we ain't very careful."

"You ain't goin' to spend it all, Narcissa!" William gave a little gasp in spite of himself.

"Land, no! We couldn't, unless we stayed three years. But—I shouldn't be surprised if it took 'most a year to spend what I've laid out to."

" 'Most a year!"

"Yes; I've got to buy us both new clothes. We ain't neither of us got anything fit to wear, and ain't had for years. We didn't go to the funeral looking decent, and I know folks talked. Mother felt bad about it, but I wasn't going to lay out money foolish and get things here when I was going to New York. I'm going to buy us some jewelry too. Father never even bought Mother a ring when they were married. I ain't saying anything against him; it wasn't the fashion so much in those days."

"I was calculatin'—" William stammered, blushing. "I always meant to, Narcissa."

"There's another thing I'm going to have, too, an' that's a gold watch. I've wanted one all my life."

"Mebbe—" began William painfully.

"No! I don't want you to buy me one. I ain't ever thought of it. I'm going to buy it myself. I'm going to buy Mother a real nice shawl, too, like the one that New York lady had who came to visit Lawyer Maxham's wife. I've got a list of things written down on paper."

Soon the news that Narcissa and her mother were going to New York was abroad. On the morning they started, all the windows were set with peering faces.

"Ten chances to one Narcissa'll pick up somebody down in New York, with all that money. She's good-lookin', and she looks better since her father died," the women told one another.

Narcissa, riding out of her native village, said not a word, but looked ahead with shining eyes.

"S'pose we shan't see you back in these parts for some time," the stage driver said, when he helped them out at the railroad station. He was an old man, and had known Narcissa since her childhood.

"Most likely not," she replied.

"Well, I'll be on the lookout for you a year from to-day."

Over and over, his brain worked the thought. "Narcissa Stone an' her mother are goin' to be gone a year afore I'll drive 'em home."

So fixed was his mind upon that outcome that when Narcissa and her mother reappeared in less than one week—in six days—he could not for a moment bring his mind to bear upon it.

For a second he had a bewildered feeling that time had flown fast, that a week was a year. He would scarcely have known them. Mrs. Stone wore a fine black satin gown; her old face looked out of fur and lace and rich black plumage. As for Narcissa, she was almost royal. The old stage driver backed and ducked awkwardly, as if she were a stranger, when she approached.

Then he said, doubtfully, bringing one white-browed eye to bear over his shoulder, "Didn't stay quite so long as you calculated on?"

"No, we didn't," replied Narcissa, calmly.

The stage passed William Crane's house.

"We've got home," said Narcissa.

William nodded; he could not speak.

That evening, when William Crane reached his sweetheart's house, he stared at her open-mouthed. She wore a gown the like of which he had never seen—soft lengths of blue silk and lace trailed about her; blue ribbons fluttered.

"What started you home so soon?"

"I spent—all the money."

"All that money! Fifteen hundred dollars in less'n a week?"

"I spent more'n that."

Narcissa was pale, but she spoke decidedly. "I'm going to tell you just what I've been doing; then you can make up your mind.

"We got to New York Thursday night and went to a beautiful hotel. The ceilin' had pictures on it. There was a handsome young gentleman downstairs at a counter in the room where we went first.

"He said—he was real polite—if we had any money, he would put it in the safe. So we did. Then a young man with brass buttons on his coat showed us our rooms. We had a parlor with a velvet carpet an' stuffed furniture and a gilt clock, two bedrooms, and a bathroom. There ain't anything in town equal to it. Lawyer Maxham ain't got anything to come up to it.

"The first morning Mother an' me went out real early. I got Mother an' me, first of all, two handsome black silk dresses, and we put 'em on as soon as we got back to the hotel, and went down to breakfast.

"You never see anythin' like the dining room, and the kinds of things to eat.

"Then we went out again. Mother an' me never had any Christmas presents, an' I told her we'd begin an' buy 'em. When the money I'd taken with us was gone, I sent things to the hotel for the gentleman at the counter to pay, the way he'd told me to. That day we bought breastpins and this ring, an' Mother's and my gold watches, an'—I got one for you, too, William. Don't you say anything—it's your Christmas present. That evenin' we went to the theater. The next day we went to the stores again, an' I bought Mother a black satin dress, and me a green one. I got a hat, too, an' a fur cape, and Mother a cloak with fur on the neck.

"The next day was Sunday. Mother an' me went to a splendid church. Everywhere we went we rode in a carriage. They invited us to at the hotel, an' I s'posed it was free.

"The next day was Monday—that's yesterday. Mother an' me went out to the stores again. We were goin' to the theater in the evening; but the gentleman at the counter called out to me when I was going past an' said he wanted to speak to me a minute.

"Then I found out we'd spent all that fifteen hundred dollars, an' more, too. We owed 'em ten dollars at the hotel; an' that wa'n't the worst of it—we didn't have enough money to take us home.

"Mother, she broke right down an' cried. Folks came crowding round. A lady came an' held a smelling bottle to my nose.

"I told 'em the whole story—about Father an' his illness an' everything. They said the rest of our bill to them was no matter, an' they gave us our tickets to come home."

There was a pause.

"I went an' wasted fifteen hundred dollars. I've had one good time, an'—I ain't sorry. You can do just what you think best, William, an'—I won't blame you."

William's eyes were full of tears. His wide mouth was trembling. "Do you think you can be contented to—stay on my side of the wall now, Narcissa?"

Narcissa in her blue robes went over to him and put, for the first time of her own will, an arm around his faithful neck. "I wouldn't go out again if the bars were down," said she.

THE BET

by Anton Chekhov

It was a dark autumn night. The old banker was pacing from corner to corner of his study, recalling to his mind the party he gave in the autumn fifteen years before. There were many clever people at the party and much interesting conversation. They talked among other things of capital punishment. The guests for the most part disapproved of it. Some of them thought that capital punishment should be replaced universally by life imprisonment.

"I don't agree with you," said the host. "I myself have experienced neither capital punishment nor life imprisonment, but in my opinion capital punishment is more moral and more humane than imprisonment. Execution kills instantly; life imprisonment kills by degrees. Who is the more humane executioner, one who kills you in a few seconds or one who draws the life out of you slowly, for years?"

"They're both equally immoral," remarked one of the guests, "because their purpose is the same, to take away life."

Among the company was a lawyer, a young man of about twenty-five. On being asked his opinion, he said: "Capital punishment and life imprisonment are equally immoral; but if I were offered the choice between them, I would certainly choose the second. It's better to live somehow than not to live at all."

There followed a lively discussion. The banker, who was then younger and more nervous, suddenly lost his temper, banged his fist on the table, and turning to the young lawyer, cried out: "It's a lie. I bet you two millions you wouldn't stick in a cell even for five years."

"If you mean it seriously," replied the lawyer, "then I bet I'll stay not five but fifteen."

"Fifteen! Done!" cried the banker. "Gentlemen, I stake two millions."

"Agreed. You stake two millions, I my freedom," said the lawyer.

So this wild, ridiculous bet came to pass. The banker, who at that time had too many millions to count, was overjoyed.

And now, pacing from corner to corner, the banker recalled all this and asked himself: "Why did I make this bet? What's the good? The lawyer loses fifteen years of his life, and I throw away two millions. Will it convince people that capital punishment is worse than imprisonment for life?"

He recollected further what happened after the evening party. It was decided that the lawyer must undergo his imprisonment under the strictest observation, in a garden wing of the banker's house. It was agreed that during the period he would be deprived of the right to cross the threshold, to see living people, to hear human voices, and to receive letters and newspapers. He was permitted to have a musical instrument, to read books, to write letters, to drink wine and smoke tobacco. By the agreement, he could communicate, but only in silence, with the outside world through a little window. Everything necessary, books, music, wine, he could receive in any quantity by sending a note through the window. The agreement obliged the lawyer to remain exactly fifteen years from twelve o'clock of November 14th, 1870, to twelve o'clock of November 14th, 1885. The least attempt on his part to violate the conditions, to escape if only for two minutes before the time, freed the banker from the obligation to pay him the two millions.

During the first year of imprisonment, the lawyer, as far as it was possible to judge from his short notes, suffered terribly from loneliness and boredom. From his wing day and night came the sound of the piano. He rejected wine and tobacco. He read books of a light character.

In the second year, the piano was heard no longer, and the lawyer asked only for classics. In the fifth year, music was heard again, and the prisoner asked for wine. Those who watched him said that during the whole of that year he was only eating, drinking, and lying on his bed. He yawned often and talked angrily to himself. Books he did not read. Sometimes at night he would sit down to write. He would write for a long time and tear it all up in the morning. More than once he was heard to weep.

In the second half of the sixth year, the prisoner began to study languages and history. He fell on these subjects so hungrily that the banker hardly had time to get books enough for him. In the space of four years, about six hundred volumes were bought at his request.

Later on, after the tenth year, the lawyer sat motionless before his table and read only the New Testament. The banker found it strange that a man who in four years had mastered six hundred volumes should have spent nearly a year in reading one book, easy to understand and by no means thick. The New Testament was then replaced by the history of religions.

During the last two years of his confinement, the prisoner read an extraordinary amount, quite haphazardly. Now he would apply himself to the natural sciences, then he would read Byron or Shakespeare. Notes used to come from him in which he asked to be sent at the same time a book on chemistry, a textbook of medicine, a novel, and some volume on ideas or religion. He read as though he were swimming in the sea among broken pieces of wreckage, and in his desire to save his life was eagerly grasping one piece after another.

The banker recalled all this, and thought: "Tomorrow at twelve o'clock he receives his freedom. Under the agreement, I shall have to pay him two millions. If I pay, it's all over with me. I am ruined forever . . ."

Fifteen years before he had too many millions to count, but now he was afraid to ask himself which he had more of, money or debts. He had become an ordinary banker, trembling at every rise and fall in the market.

"That cursed bet," murmured the old man, clutching his head in despair. "The only escape from bankruptcy and disgrace—is that the man should die!"

The clock had just struck three. The banker was listening. In the house everyone was alseep, and one could hear only the frozen trees whining outside the windows. Trying to make no sound, he took out of his safe the key of the door that had not been opened for fifteen years, put on his overcoat, and went out of the house. The garden was dark and cold. It was raining. A damp, penetrating wind howled in the garden and gave the trees no rest. Approaching the garden wing, he called the watchman twice. There was no answer.

"If I have the courage to fulfill my intention," thought the old man, "the suspicion will fall on the watchman first of all."

In the darkness he groped for the steps and the door and poked his way into a narrow passage and struck a match. Not a soul was there. The seals on the door that led into the prisoner's room were unbroken.

When the match went out, the old man, trembling from agitation, peeped into the little window.

In the prisoner's room a candle was burning dimly. The prisoner himself sat by the table. Only his back, the hair on his head, and his hands were visible. Open books were scattered about on the table, the two chairs, and on the carpet near the table.

Five minutes passed and the prisoner never once stirred. The banker tapped on the window with his finger, but the prisoner made no movement in reply. Then the banker cautiously tore the seals from the door and put the key into the lock. The rusty lock gave a hoarse groan and the door creaked. The banker expected instantly to hear a cry of surprise and the sound of steps. Three minutes passed and it was as quiet inside as it had been before. He made up his mind to enter.

Before the table sat a man, unlike an ordinary human being. It was a skeleton, with tight-drawn skin, with long curly hair like a woman's, and a shaggy beard. The color of his face was yellow, of an earthy shade; the cheeks were sunken, the back long and narrow, and the hand upon which he leaned his hairy head was so lean and skinny that it was painful to look upon. His hair was already silvering with gray, and no one who looked upon the face would have believed that he was only forty years old. On the table, before his bended head, lay a sheet of paper.

"Poor devil," thought the banker, "he's asleep and probably seeing millions in his dreams. I have only to take and throw this half-dead thing on the bed, smother him a moment with the pillow, and the most careful examination will find no trace of unnatural death. But, first, let us read what he has written here."

The banker took the sheet from the table and read:

"Tomorrow I shall obtain my freedom and the right to mix with people. But before I leave this room and see the sun, I think it necessary to say a few words to you. I declare to you that I despise freedom, life, health, and all that your books call the blessings of the world.

"For fifteen years I have thoroughly studied earthly life. True, I saw neither the earth nor the people, but in your books I drank fragrant wine, sang songs, hunted deer in the forests, loved women. In your books I climbed lofty mountains and saw from there the way the sun rose in the morning. I saw the mountain ridges touched with a purple gold. I saw green forests, fields, rivers, lakes, and cities. In your books I cast myself into bottomless pits, worked miracles, burned cities to the ground, preached new religions, conquered whole countries.

"Your books gave me wisdom. All that human thought created over centuries is condensed to a little lump in my skull. I know that I am cleverer than you all.

"And I despise your books, despise all worldly blessings and wisdom. Though you be proud and wise and beautiful, yet will death wipe you from the face of the earth.

"You are mad, and gone the wrong way. You take falsehood for truth and ugliness for beauty.

"That I may show you in deed my contempt for that by which you live, I will refuse the two millions, of which I once dreamed as of paradise, and which I now despise. That I may deprive myself of my right to them, I shall come out from here five minutes before the term ends, and thus shall violate the agreement."

When he had finished reading, the banker put the sheet on the table, kissed the head of the strange man, and began to weep. He went out of the wing. Never at any other time had he felt such contempt for himself as now. Coming home, he lay down on his bed, but agitation and tears kept him a long time from sleeping.

The next morning the poor watchman came running to him and told him that they had seen the man who lived in the wing climb through the window into the garden. He had gone to the gate and disappeared. The banker instantly went with his servant to the wing and established the escape of his prisoner. To avoid unnecessary rumors, he took the paper with the statement from the table and, on his return, locked it in his safe.

The Last Shot

by Darcy Frey

Russell Thomas places his right sneaker one inch behind the three-point line, considers the basket with a level gaze, draws back his wrist to shoot, then suddenly looks around. He is lifting his nose to the wind like a spaniel; he is gauging air currents. He waits until the wind settles, bits of trash feathering lightly to the ground. Then he sends a twenty-five-foot jump shot arcing through the soft summer twilight. It drops without a sound through the dead center of the bare iron rim. So does the next one. So does the one after that. Alone in the gathering dusk, Russell works the perimeter against imaginary defenders, making jump shots from all points. Few sights on Brooklyn playgrounds stir the hearts and minds of coaches and scouts who recruit young men for college basketball teams quite like Russell's jumper. But the shot is merely the final gesture, the public flourish of a private routine that brings Russell to this court day and night. Avoiding pickup games, he gets down to work: an hour of three-point shooting, then wind sprints up the fourteen flights of stairs in his project, then back to the court, where (much to his friends' amusement) he shoots one-handers ten feet from the basket while sitting in a chair.

At this hour Russell usually has the court to himself; most of the other players won't come out until after dark, when the thick humid air begins to stir with night breezes and the court lights come on. But this evening is turning out to be a fine one—cool and foggy. The low, slanting sun sheds a feeble pink light over the silvery Atlantic a block away, and milky sheets of fog roll off the ocean and drift in tatters along the project walkways. The air smells of sewage and saltwater. At the far end of the court, where someone has torn a hole in the chicken-wire fence, other players climb through and begin warming up.

Like most of New York's poverty-stricken and principally black neighborhoods, Coney Island does not exactly shower its youth with opportunity. In the early 1960s, the city built a vast tract of housing projects in Coney Island, packed so densely along a twenty-block stretch that a new skyline rose suddenly behind the boardwalk and amusement park. The experiment of public housing, which has isolated the nation's poor from the hearts of their cities, may have failed here in even more spectacular fashion because of Coney Island's utter remoteness. In this neighborhood, on a peninsula at the southern tip of Brooklyn, there are almost no stores, no trees, no police; just block after block of gray cement projects—looming, prison-like, and jutting straight into the sea.

Most summer nights a vague unease settles over Coney Island as apartments become too stifling to bear and the streets fall prey to the gangs and drug dealers. Officially, Coney Island is deemed to be a part of the endless rapidly changing scene that is New York City. But on nights like these, as the dealers set up their drug markets in the streets and alleyways, and the sounds of sirens and gunfire keep pace with the darkening sky, it feels like the end of the world. Yet even in Coney Island there are some uses to which a young man's talent, ambition, and desire to stay out of harm's way may be put: there is basketball. Hidden behind the projects are dozens of courts, and every night they fill with restless teenagers, there to remain for hours until exhaustion or the street toughs take over.

The neighborhood's best players—the ones like Russell, with aspirations—practice a disciplined, team-driven style of basketball at this court by the O'Dwyer projects, which has been named the Garden after the New York Knicks' arena. In a neighborhood overrun by the commerce of drugs, the Garden offers a slight sanctuary. A few years ago, community leaders petitioned the housing authority to install night lights. And the players themselves renovated the court and put up regulation-height rims that snap back after a player dunks[1]. Russell may be the only kid at the Garden conscientious enough to practice his footwork while holding a ten-pound brick in each hand, but no one here treats the game as child's play. Even the toughs decline to vandalize the Garden, because in Coney Island the possibility of excelling through basketball is an article of faith.

The notion that basketball can liberate dedicated players like these from the grinding daily hardships of the ghetto has become a cherished myth, advanced by television sportscasters, college basketball publicity agents, and sneaker companies

[1]Dunks: Throws the ball down through the basket from above the rim.

selling hard work and $120 high-tops. And that myth is conveyed directly to the players at the Garden by the dozens of college coaches who arrive in Coney Island each year with assurances that even if a National Basketball Association contract isn't in the cards, a player's talent and determination will at least reward him with a free college education, a decent job, and a one-way ticket out of the neighborhood. But how often is basketball's promise of a better life fulfilled?

"Just do it, right?" It is Corey Johnson, smiling mischievously, eyes luminous. He nods toward the court—players stretching out, taking lay-up shots—and it does, in fact, resemble a sneaker commercial. Corey is a skillful mimic and he does a superb white TV announcer. "These sneakers get you where you want to go, which is out of the ghetto!" He laughs.

Corey is Russell's best friend and one of Lincoln High's other star seniors. He, too, expects to play college ball. But he indulges in witty indifference and normally shows up courtside with his Walkman merely to watch for girls beneath his handsome, hooded eyes. He loops his fingers around the chicken-wire fence and says, "I tell you, Coney Island is like a disease. Of the mind. It makes you lazy. You relax too much. 'Cause all you ever see is other guys relaxing."

Although a pickup game has begun at the basket nearest Corey, Russell still commands the other. Corey smiles at his friend's laborious discipline. Russell, it is hoped, will play next year in the Big East, one of the nation's top college conferences. Russell is six feet three, 180 pounds, with a shaved head and a small pointed, trimmed beard that seems to mean business. But one can never predict what may happen to Russell, because, as Corey observes, “Russell is Russell.” I can guess what this means: Russell lives in one of the neighborhood’s toughest projects, and misfortune often seems to shadow him. Last year a fight between Russell and his girlfriend turned violent. Terrified that his scholarship[2] had just been replaced by a stiff prison term, Russell climbed to the top of one of Coney Island’s highest buildings. It took almost half an hour of reasoned talk by his high-school coach and members of the Sixtieth Precinct to bring him back from the edge.[3]

Russell may be tightly wound, but no Coney Island player can avoid for long the intense pressures that might bring a teenager with his whole life ahead of him to the edge of a roof. Basketball newsletters and scouting reports are constantly examining the players, and practically every day some coach shows up—judging, coaxing, bargaining, and, as often as not, making promises he never keeps. Getting that scholarship offer is every player’s dream—in anticipation, no one steps outside in Coney Island without a Syracuse cap or a St. John’s sweatshirt. But in reality only a handful of the neighborhood’s players have ever made it to such top four-year programs; most have been turned back by one obstacle or another in high school. Others who have enrolled in college never saw their dream to completion.

[2]Scholarship: Grant of money to help a student continue his or her studies.

[3]Because of this incident, Russell’s name has been changed in this article.

The orange court lights have come on now, displacing the invading darkness. Two players on either end of the court climb the fence and sit on top of the backboards, hanging nets—a sign that a serious game is about to begin. Suddenly a ferocious grinding noise fills the air. It gets louder and louder, and then a teenage kid riding a Big Wheel careens onto the court. He darts through the playground crowd, then hops off his ride and watches it slam into the fence. "Ah, yes, Stephon Marbury," Corey says dryly, "future of the neighborhood."

Stephon is barely fourteen, has yet to begin high school, but already his recruiting has begun. At least one college coach is known to have sent him fawning letters in violation of National Collegiate Athletic Association rules; street agents, paid under the table by colleges to bring top players to their programs, have begun cultivating Stephon; and practically every high-school coach in the city is heaping him with free gear—sneakers, caps, bags—in an attempt to lure him to his school. At first glance, Stephon doesn't look like the future of anything: he's small, barely five feet nine, with the rounded forehead and delicate features of an infant.

With Stephon here, Corey wanders onto the court. Russell, too, is persuaded to give up his solo practice session. Basketball, it is commonly said, is a game of pure instinct, but the five-on-five contest that begins here is something else. Corey and Stephon are cousins, and Russell is as good as family—the three of them have played together since they were in grade school. They seem to move as if the instinctive magical geometry of the game had all been rehearsed in advance. Stephon, the smallest by far, is doing tricks with the ball as though it were dangling from his hand by a string, then gunning it to his older teammates with a series of expert no-look passes: behind-the-back passes, sidearm passes, shovel passes. Corey is lulling defenders with his sleepy eyes, then exploding to the basket, where he casually tosses the ball through the hoop. Russell is sinking twenty-footers with ease.

The game has just begun when a crowd starts to form: sidelined players, three deep, waiting their turn. A drunk yells, "I played with Jordan, I played with Jabbar. They're no big deal. And neither are *you*!" A guy in a silk suit and alligator shoes arrives. An agent? A scout? The crowd gives him elbow room. A couple of young mothers with strollers come by; they get less elbow room.

Basketball is so tightly woven into the fabric of Coney Island life that almost everyone here can recite a complete oral history of the neighborhood's players. People remember the exact scores of summer tournament games played at this court ten years ago, or describe in elated detail the perfect arc that Carlton "Silk" Owens put on his jumper before he was shot in the elbow in 1982.

Russell, Corey, and Stephon are the natural heirs to this lofty tradition. But this is a complicated business: given the failures that have preceded them, the new crew is watched by the neighborhood with a certain timidity, a growing reluctance to care too deeply. Yet Coney Island offers its residents little else on which to hang their pride. So the proceedings here take on a desperate, elevated quality, and by unspoken agreement the misfortunes of bygone players are chalked up to either a lack of will or plain bad luck—both of which make possible the survival of hope.

It's past midnight now, and the encompassing glow of Manhattan's remote skyscrapers has turned the sky a metallic blue. Standing courtside, we can see only the darkened outlines of the projects, looming in every direction, and the shirtless players streaking back and forth, drenched in a pool of orange light. For Russell, Corey, and Stephon, the hard labor of winning their scholarships lies ahead; for now this game is enough. Corey, sprinting downcourt, calls out, "Homeboy! Homeboy!" Standing under his own basket, Stephon lets fly with a long, unlikely pass that Corey somehow manages to catch and dunk in one graceful leap. The game is stopped on account of chaos: players and spectators are screaming and staggering around the court—knees buckling, heads held in astonishment. Stephon laughs and points to the rim, still shuddering fearfully from its run-in with Corey's fists. "Yo, cuz," he yells. "Make it bleed!" Then he raises his arms jubilantly and does a little dance, rendered momentarily insane by the sheer dizzying pleasure of playing this game to perfection.

The Youngest Miss Piper

by Bret Harte

None of us eligible bachelors from Red Gulch who knew the Piper girls ever cared much for the youngest sister. It wasn't that she was boring; she seemed much more witty than others her age. Nor was she hard to get along with, as she not only had a good sense of humor but had an open personality that let you know where you stood. And it wasn't because of her slight deafness, which sometimes made us say things too loudly that we would rather have whispered behind closed doors. Briefly, it was very possible that Delaware, the youngest Miss Piper, did not like us.

We gathered from her disdain that the youngest Miss Piper was impervious to general masculine advances, and so were astonished by the rumors that all this time she really had a lover! We were particularly sensitive to the fact that her deafness did not prevent her from perfectly understanding the ordinary tone of voice of a certain Mr. Thomas Sparrell.

At first we didn't consider it a matter of great consequence. Sparrell, a lanky, red-haired youth unable to do manual labor because of a lame leg, was a clerk in the general store at the crossroads. He had never been a guest at Judge Piper's home; he had never even delivered packages to the house. To our knowledge, his only interviews with Delaware had been over the counter at the store. In short, Thomas Sparrell was the last man we would have expected her to select as an admirer.

To see them in public you would guess that their relationship was "strictly business." Of course, there was a lot of business being carried on because Del was in charge of provisioning the Piper household. The following is said to be a truthful record of one of their exchanges overhead at the store:

"I admire having conversations with you, Mr. Sparrell; it's better than a circus. I suppose you get all your information out of books," indicating a volume concealed under the counter. "What do you call that one?"

Sparrell (politely): *"The First Principles of Geology."*

Miss Delaware: "Did you say the first principles of 'geology' or 'grocery'? Whichever it is, you make it sound a most interesting topic. Well, it's too bad folks can't just spend their lives listening to such elegant talk. I'd admire to do nothing else! But there's my family up at Cottonwood—and they must eat. They're that low that they expect me to waste my time getting food for them here, instead of drinking in *The First Principles of the Grocery.*"

"Geology," suggested Sparrell patiently. "The history of rock formation."

"Geology," accepted Miss Delaware, "the history of rocks. Thank you for a most improving afternoon, Mr. Sparrell," and she sailed coyly out of the store.

Some people thought it odd that a daughter of Judge Piper should spend so much time rubbing elbows with a clerk at the general store. But certainly no one ever dreamed that those meetings pointed to any more intimate confidences between them.

I think the secret burst upon the family, along with other things, at the big picnic at Reservoir Canyon. The in crowd of Red Gulch had been planning it for weeks. The site selected was a beautiful triangular valley with very steep sides, one of which was crowned by the immense reservoir of the Pioneer Ditch Company.

Reservoir Canyon seemed an ideal place for a picnic. Everybody was therefore astonished to hear that an objection was suddenly raised to this perfect site. They were even more astonished to know that the objector was the youngest Miss Piper! Pressed to give her reasons, she had replied that the locality was dangerous. She said that the walls of the reservoir were notoriously old and worn-out, and that they had been rendered more dangerous by the false economy of unskillful and hasty repairs to satisfy speculating stockbrokers. She added that it had shown signs of leaking, and that in the event of an outbreak, the triangular valley would be instantly flooded. Asked to give her authority for these details, she gave the name of—Tom Sparrell.

No one was surprised when we laughed at her statements. What was surprising was the anger expressed by Judge Piper. It was not generally known that the judge owned a considerable number of shares in the Pioneer Ditch Company, and that he had been in on the shady deals that resulted in the faulty repair of the reservoir walls. He and the other speculators stood to make a lot of money by selling out the stock of a failing company to unsuspecting buyers. Everyone believed that the judge's anger was due only to the discovery of Sparrell's influence over his daughter. There was a nasty scene between the youngest Miss Piper and the combined forces of her father and older sisters, which ended in Delaware's absolute refusal to attend the picnic at all if they intended to have it at Reservoir Canyon.

Her warning was conspicuously ineffective. Everyone eagerly looked forward to the day and the unchanged locality. When at last the appointed hour had arrived, the picnic party passed down the twisting mountain in a fever of enthusiasm.

Two hours had passed in dancing and games when the party sat down for the long-anticipated meal. Suddenly, half a dozen picnickers started to their feet.

"What is it?" everyone was asking with questioning looks.

It was Judge Piper who replied.

"Just a little shock of earthquake," he said without much excitement in his voice.

He was interrupted by a faint crashing and crackling sound, and looking up saw a good-sized boulder bounding into the forest. Then a scream from Georgia Piper attracted everyone's attention. She was standing on a picnic bench, staring at the top of the trail. "Look!" she said excitedly, "that trail is moving!"

Everyone faced in that direction. At first glance it seemed as if the trail was actually moving, wriggling its way down the mountain like a huge snake swollen to twice its usual size. But the second glance showed it to be no longer a trail but a channel of water four or five feet high, plunging down into the valley.

For an instant they were unable to comprehend the nature of the catastrophe. The reservoir was directly over their heads. If the wall did burst, they had imagined that the water would come down in a dozen trickling streams over the cliff above them. But that it should descend in a raging flood by their own trail and their only avenue of escape had been beyond their wildest imagination.

When the flood struck, it wiped the picnic off the face of the earth in about twenty-five seconds! It was at this point that the situation became really desperate, for the picnickers had now crawled up the steep sides as far as the bushes afforded foothold, and the water was still rising. The men discussed the wildest plans, such as tearing their shirts into strips to make ropes to support the women by sticks driven into the mountainside.

Suddenly, the distinct strokes of a woodman's ax were heard high at the point where the trail descended to the canyon. Every ear was alert, but only those on one side of the canyon could get a view of the spot. Georgia Piper, who had climbed to the highest point on that side, was now standing bolt upright and gesturing excitedly in that direction.

"Someone is cutting down a tree at the head of the trail," she shouted. The joyful explanation, "for a dam across the trail," was on everybody's lips at the same time.

But the strokes of the ax were painfully slow. Impatience burst out.

"Yell to him to hurry up! Why haven't they brought two men?"

"It's only one man," shouted Georgia, "and he seems to be having trouble wielding the ax. It looks like—it is—yes—it's Tom Sparrell!"

The blows still went on slowly. Presently, however, they seemed to alternate with other blows. Georgia continued to describe the scene. "It's a woman. Why, sure as you live, it's Delaware!"

A cheer burst from the group.

Still the blows went on at a distressingly slow speed. The picnickers were more than half submerged. There was a painful pause, then a crumbling crash. Another cheer went up from the canyon.

"It's down—straight across the trail," shouted Georgia, "and a part of the bank on top of it."

There was another moment of suspense. Would it hold or be carried away by the force of the flood? It held! In a few moments the flow had stopped and the submerged trail reappeared. In twenty minutes it was clear—a muddy river bed, but possible of ascent! Of course there was still water in the canyon, but it now was possible for the party to swing from bush to bush along the mountainside until the trail was reached.

There were some missteps and mishaps, flounderings in the water, and some dangerous rescues, but in half an hour everyone stood upon the trail and commenced the ascent. It was a slow and difficult procession. When they reached the dam made by the fallen tree, they could see how successfully it had diverted the direction of the current.

But strangely enough, they were greeted by nothing else! Sparrell and Delaware were gone, and when they at last reached the high road, they were astounded to hear from a passerby that no one in the village knew anything of the disaster!

That was the last straw. They had expected that everyone would be waiting breathlessly for their rescue. They had anticipated that they would be welcomed as heroes. Instead, they were obliged to meet the ill-concealed amusement of all their friends at their untidy and bedraggled appearance, which suggested only the blundering mishaps of an ordinary summer outing! The fleeting sense of gratitude they had felt for their rescuers was gone by the time they had reached their homes, and their annoyance increased when they heard that when the earthquake occurred Mr. Tom Sparrell and Miss Delaware were enjoying a walk in the forest—he having a half holiday because of the picnic—and that the earthquake had revived his fears of a catastrophe. The two had obtained axes in the woodman's hut and did what they thought was necessary to relieve the situation of the picnickers.

For the first time in the history of Red Gulch, there was a serious division between the Piper family and the rest of the town. The latter remembered Tom Sparrell's warning and commented on the ingratitude of the picnickers to their rescuers.

There was also a stormy scene in the Piper household itself. The judge had demanded that Delaware break off her relationship with Sparrell. She had refused. The judge had demanded of Sparrell's employer that he discharge him and had been met with the astounding information that Sparrell had worked his way up into being a partner in the concern. He made a final appeal to Delaware. He implored her to consider the situation of her sisters who had all made more ambitious marriages or were about to make them.

Here the youngest Miss Piper made a memorable reply.

"You all want to know why I'm going to marry Tom Sparrell?" she inquired, facing the whole family circle.

"Yes."

"Why I prefer him to any of the bunch that you girls have married or are going to marry?" she continued.

"Yes."

"Well, he's the only man of the whole lot that can stand on his own two feet and do his own thinking."

They were married that autumn. A later comparison of family records showed that the other sons-in-law did not advance proportionately in standing or riches, while the lame storekeeper of Red Gulch became the Honorable Senator Tom Sparrell.

See No Evil

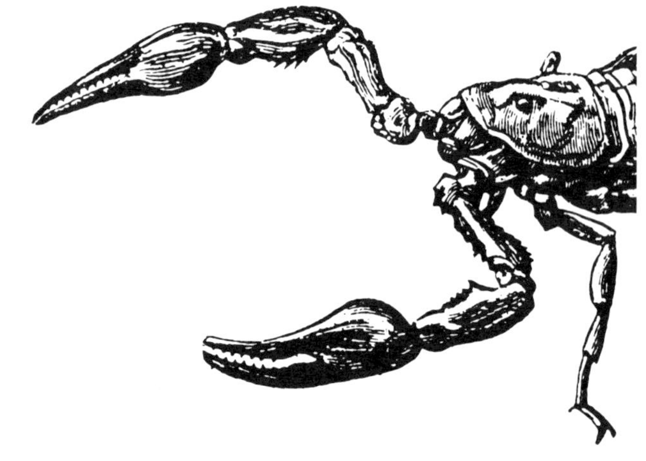
HART PICTURE ARCHIVES

Allow me to confess a disturbing personal bias: I don't trust any animal with more than six legs and more than two eyes. No explanation for this, just a reflex from my subconcious, but there you are. Six and two. I go sick with terror and disgust whenever confronted with a beast who violates those magic limits. Six and two. Insects,

by David Quammen

however strange, are fine. Snakes are among my favorite living things—beautiful, sleek, unadorned, binocular.

A dizzying wave of sickness passes over me, on the other hand, at the very glimpse of a color photograph of a black widow spider. One, two, three, four, five, six, seven, yuk eight, and then the legs. Am I alone or does anyone else feel this way? Raise your hands, please. Have you ever looked a black widow spider closely in the face? Poison isn't the problem; a rattlesnake has poison, yet a rattlesnake is merely handsome and dangerous. I know it's unfair, but a creature with that many legs and eyes, you just never know what it might be getting ready to do. One on one, it already has you surrounded. Spiders are bad enough. Consider, though, the scorpion.

My own heartfelt conviction is that scorpions are perhaps the most disgusting group of animals on the face of the earth, even including toy poodles. Maybe that's part of what makes them so interesting. Scorpions violate the six-and-two rule conspicuously: four pairs of walking legs, one pair of grasping claws, one pair of leglike limbs modified to serve as jaws, another pair that are hidden beneath the abdomen like landing gear and perform some still-mysterious function—14 limbs altogether—plus anywhere from zero to 12 eyes, but in most species eight, arranged in three widely spaced clusters like movie cameras. As if that weren't enough, they also carry a nasty stinger hanging overhead on the end of a long tail, like a sharpened spear ready to plunge. Scorpions are more cluttered with useful hardware than a Swiss Army knife.

They travel under cover of darkness. They prey on insects and spiders, as well as on occasional small lizards or mice. They kill people too, surprisingly many in some countries—though only while defending themselves, or by mistake. A scorpion drops from the roof of a house into a baby's crib, a young child runs barefoot through a garden, an adult carelessly picks up a piece of firewood, and whammo. In Mexico, at least until recently, more than a thousand humans died each year from scorpion stings. Most of those victims were kids. Another 69,000

Mexicans annually survive a sting that is at least bad enough to report. Scorpions can be found nearly everywhere in the warm latitudes, in jungles and mountains as well as deserts; but among the different species there is wide variation in the strength of the venom.

Some venoms merely cause local swelling and pain. Others attack the nervous system, resulting in high pulse rate, irregular breathing, feeling of fright or excitement, impaired vision, vomiting, and a range of other symptoms of which the final, if it comes to that, is complete respiratory failure. Death by suffocation, out there under the clear tropical sky.

J.L. Cloudsley-Thompson, a British scientist who spent part of his career as a museum keeper, described the whole sequence: "First, a feeling of tightness develops in the throat so that the victim tries to clear his throat. The tongue develops a feeling of thickness and speech becomes difficult. The victim next becomes restless and there may be slight, involuntary twitching of the muscles. Small children at this stage will not be still: Some attempt to climb up the wall or the sides of the cot. Repeated sneezing is accompanied by a continuous flow of fluid from nose and mouth. Occasionally the rate of heartbeat is considerably increased. Convulsions follow, the arms are waved about, and the limbs become quite blue before death occurs."

Cloudsley-Thompson might be talking about a sting from the fearsome North African species said to have extremely toxic venom, but he isn't. He's talking about an American scorpion called the bark scorpion. The bark scorpion gets its name from its habit of hiding beneath loose and fallen pieces of tree bark. During one 20-year period, it accounted for 64 deaths in just the state of Arizona.

The Cloudsley-Thompson description and the number of deaths in Arizona may both be unduly alarming. The bark scorpion is quite common in Arizona, and many people are stung by it without suffering any ill effects. One of those victims, Steve Prchal of the Arizona-Sonora Desert Museum near Tucson, describes the experience this way: "Take a sharp needle and jab it into your hand. Hold a match or a lighter to it for a couple of hours. Then add the needles-and-pins sensation you have when a foot falls asleep. That's what a bark scorpion sting feels like." Evidently, the reaction can range anywhere from modest discomfort to horrible death, depending upon body size and general health of the person stung, as well as other factors, including luck. Best to steer clear of scorpion neighborhoods, then, when you feel especially frail or unlucky.

Steve Prchal got his sting during a family camping trip, five minutes after having warned the other family members to be careful of scorpions. He reached for a boat cushion that had been drying on top of a bus. Whammo. That pattern seems to be typical. But considering both the number of scorpions and the number of people at large in the state of Arizona, sting incidents don't happen nearly so often as they might. What makes scorpions a threat to people is no special nastiness on the part of the scorpions but the fact that, because of their shyness, you don't see them until it's too late.

They hide during the day, under bark or in rocky crevices, emerging at night to hunt. If you have ever lain down in a sleeping bag on the warm Arizona earth, you have probably had a closer encounter with these creatures than you realized. And yet, because you can't see them, you might well conclude they aren't really there. To see them at night, shine a blacklight beam on them and (due to properties of the scorpion shell about which little seems to be known) they reflect back a greenish-blue glow. A dreamlike image in bright neon except that the animal, and the sting, are quite real.

Steve Prchal designed the live-scorpion exhibits at the Desert Museum. He tells of going out on collecting trips. Like many collectors, he went at night and used a black-light flashlight, shinning his invisible beam along the walls of a dry creek bed. "It was like stars," Prchal says. "It would scare the heck out of you to see how many you'd be sleeping with if you camped there." He didn't camp there, because he was too smart. I wasn't, when I lived in those parts, so I did. Saw not a single scorpion.

Curious about how others have fared among the scorpions of the Arizona desert, I decided to consult a couple of graduate student desert rats. First I called Doug Peacock, an authority on the wild behavior of bears and humans. Peacock has collected three stings, and remembers them all rather vividly. The first time was the worst. He was tucked into his sleeping bag, somewhere out in the desert, and in the middle of the night he chanced to roll over, moving one arm out blindly onto the sand. Whammo. This one may or may not have been a bark scorpion, but the local pain was ferocious and he went through a few hours of bad headache and fever. The third time, he sat down in a clearing and laid his hand back for support—right on a scorpion, which went off like a mousetrap. Perhaps it was a less poisonous species, but in this case the effects were no worse than those from a bee sting. The second time was perhaps the most interesting. Again, camping in the Arizona desert, he was sitting up late to read *Moby Dick* by the light of his campfire. He set the book down, tossed a few sticks on the fire, watched the sparks rise into black eternity, picked the book up, leaned back comfortably on an elbow, and whammo. In his anger he beat this one to death—in fact, past all chance of identification—but a reasonable bet makes it a bark scorpion.

I also talked to Ed Abbey, whose ability to speak on any matter of deserts or critters is unequaled. Amazingly, Abbey has only been scorpion-stung once, and that time while sitting quietly on a couch in a trailer house, late one night about ten years ago. He was barefoot. He was reading *Gravity's Rainbow*. He didn't notice the scorpion that had come crawling peacefully up. He lifted one foot and set it down again, whammo, but Ed was so involved in Pynchon's novel that all he recalls is smashing the scorpion to death with his stung foot, then quickly getting a bucket of ice water, jamming the foot into it, and continuing to read. Yes, he had some sharp pain at the site, definitely, but nothing much more. On the whole, says Ed, it wasn't nearly so upsetting as the time a tiny insect, species unknown, crawled deep into his ear and refused to come out.

There are several morals to be drawn. First and most obviously, heavy reading causes scorpion stings. Second, a person is safer while remaining stationary than in making even the most innocent movement—and safer still if the person remains stationary somewhere outside the borders of Arizona. And the third point to note is that the mistakes seem to be mutual: They don't see a human hand or foot coming, those scorpions, until it is too late. Otherwise they would surely, like us, prefer to avoid the entire experience.

They don't see us coming because they don't see much of anything. Strangely enough, despite their superabundance of eyes, most scorpions seem to be almost hopelessly blind. Their blindness is so pronounced, evidently, that it has been a mystery how scorpions could ever find their way to a meal. Stumbling around blindly out there in the desert, bumping into rocks and each other and Doug Peacock, the poor things should have long since starved to death and lapsed into extinction. Just lately, though, the mystery seems to have been solved. In a recent issue of *Scientific American,* Philip H. Brownell has presented impressive experimental evidence for a new theory of how scorpions sense the presence of food or danger.

They see with their feet. More precisely, they rely on pressure-sensing organs near the ends of each of their eight walking legs to sense when another creature passes by on the desert floor. Take away the input from one or two pairs of legs, or from all four legs along one side of the body, and the scorpion becomes confused. Like a human with only one good eye, and therefore no sense of depth. Take away all the input from those leg organs, and the animal is functionally blind.

They see with their feet. No wonder they need all eight. Okay, this I can accept. But I'm still uneasy about all those sparkling eyes, which seem to serve no purpose except sheer decorative vanity. Couldn't they be satisfied with just five or six?

The Unfamiliar

Part 1
by Richard Connell

Who he was and what he was and where he came from no one knew. How he came to be in Crosby Corners was a mystery. He could not speak much English beyond "Yes," "No," and "Hungry," but he could gesture—with his hands, his elbows, his eyes, his feet. He appeared to be trying by pantomime to convey the idea that he had been forcibly seized in his native land, which was remote; had been pressed into service aboard a ship; had been very ill at sea; had escaped at a port; had fled on a train; and had dropped, or been dropped, at Crosby Corners. The farmers, however, had no time to interpret pantomime. Farm hands were scarce in Connecticut, and, if a man had two hands and at least one good eye, they put him to work.

It was thus he entered the employ of Ben Crosby, richest farmer in that region.

"I found the little rascal," Ben Crosby told his wife, "frightened almost out of his wits, with Constable Pettit marching him along by the ear. The Constable says to me, 'I dunno what it is, Ben, but it looks foreign. I found it down by the railroad tracks trying to eat a raw potato.' 'Well,' I says to the Constable, 'he didn't get that tobacco-brown finish of his from working in an office. I need hands worse than ducks need ponds. Turn him over to me 'stead of sticking him in jail, and I'll give him a job.'

There he is out at the pump, washing the dirtiest pair of hands I ever saw. I'll send him to the back door, Hannah; you give him a bit of ham and eggs and pie, and then send him down to me. I'll be in the twenty-acre lot."

Mrs. Crosby opened the door and saw a small man standing there; his face was a rich brown; his eyes were black and fearful; he appeared to be ready to flee if the occasion demanded it. When he saw Mrs. Crosby, however, he bowed deeply. Such a bow had never before been executed at Crosby Corners except in the moving pictures. It was a sweeping, courtly thing, that bow, in which the small man swept off his wide felt hat and dusted the steps with it.

Then he smiled. He looked toward the stove and sighed. Mrs. Crosby pointed to a chair at the kitchen table, and he, with another bow, took it and presently was eating hungrily and freely. Mrs. Crosby now and then lifted an eye from her chores to regard the stranger; she had a doubt or two at first whether it was safe for her to stay there. She glanced into the dining room where, above the mantel, hung Grandpa Crosby's Civil War sword, a long, heavy weapon; its presence reassured her. As she studied the man, she decided that any fear of him was groundless; if anything, he was afraid of her. His hair, she observed, was blue-black and long, but arranged in a way that suggested that he was a bit of a dandy. The stranger's trousers surprised her greatly; they were of black velvet, really painfully tight, except at the bottom of each leg, where they flared out like bells. He had no belt but, instead, a scarlet sash. His silk shirt, when new and clean, must have been a remarkable garment. His boots were of patent leather and excessively pointed. He was the first man she had ever seen who walked with a dainty strut.

When Ben Crosby came in to his supper that evening he announced, "I was wrong about that new little fellow. He doesn't seem to have done farmwork. He's willing enough, but he handles a hayfork as dainty as if it was a toothpick. And he certainly is the most scary human being I ever set eyes on. You should have seen him when the tractor came into the field with the mowing machine. He gave a yelp and jumped on the stone wall, and if there'd been a tree handy, I guess he'd have climbed it. Pete High, who was driving the tractor, said, 'I guess it ain't only his skin that's yellow.' I hope Pete is wrong. I hate a coward."

"Don't you let Pete High pick on him," urged Mrs. Crosby. "Perhaps the man never saw a mowing machine before. I remember how scared I was when I saw the first automobile come roaring and snorting along the road. And so were you, Ben Crosby."

"Well, I didn't let on I was," replied her husband, harpooning a potato.

"Maybe you didn't; but I saw you looking around for a tree."

He laughed, and then they both heard a cry—a high, terrified cry that came through the dusk. He started up.

"That's not Janey?" he asked.

"No; she's still in town taking her music lesson."

"Who is it, then?"

They heard the patter of running feet on the path outside; they heard the sound of feet landing after a leap to the porch; they heard someone banging frantically on the front door. Ben Crosby called out: "What's the matter?"

A flood of words in a strange tongue answered him.

"It's Velvet Pants," he exclaimed, and flung open the door. The small man, breathless, tumbled in.

"What in the name of thunder!" demanded Ben Crosby. The small man pointed through the open door with quivering fingers.

"I don't see anything out there but the evening," said Ben Crosby.

"Ice," cried the man. "Ice!"

"What do you want ice for?" asked Ben Crosby.

The man made dramatic gestures; first he pointed at his own face, then he pointed outside; his index finger stabbed once, twice, a dozen times.

"Ice! Ice! Ice!" he said.

"Why, Ben, he means 'eyes'!" exclaimed Mrs. Crosby.

"Eyes? What eyes, Hannah? I don't see any eyes. There's nothing out there but lightning bugs."

One of the fireflies flew quite near the open door. The small man saw it coming and made an earnest, but only partly successful, attempt to climb into the grandfather's clock that stood in the corner of the hall.

Ben Crosby threw back his head and laughed.

"Why, he's afraid of lightning bugs! Hey, Velvet Pants, look here."

He captured the firefly and held it near the stranger's wide eyes.

"Look," said Ben Crosby in a loud tone. "Bug! No Hurt! Lightning bug!"

The small man pulled away from the insect.

"Not know lightnong boogs," he said.

Ben released his hold and pointed upstairs; then he gave a highly accurate imitation of a snore. The man comprehended, and his velvet-clad legs twinkled upstairs toward his bedroom. Ben Crosby returned to his supper, shaking his head.

"It beats me," he remarked to his wife. "He's afraid of mowing machines, and he's afraid of lightning bugs. I wonder if he's afraid of the dark. Can you imagine a real, honest-to-goodness farm hand like Pete High being afraid of lightning bugs?"

"Boneheads are seldom afraid of anything," remarked Mrs. Crosby, pouring buttermilk.

They heard the front door open.

Janey, daughter of the household, came in, bearing her guitar. She kissed both her parents. Janey was nearly eighteen, a pretty, elflike young woman. All the masculine hearts in Crosby Corners beat a little faster when she went down the village street; her blue eyes had been the cause of many black eyes. Her father told her of the new man, of his extraordinary velvet trousers, and of his still more extraordinary fears.

"Poor little fellow!" she said.

As the harvest days hurried along, Velvet Pants atoned somewhat for his lack of expertise as a farmer by his unfailing good nature. He even learned to speak a little English, but he had little opportunity to talk with his fellow workers. Mostly they ignored him; a man who paled at the sight of mowing machines and lightning bugs was not of their stouthearted kind.

The incident at the swimming hole added little to Velvet Pants' reputation for bravery. The swimming hole was Sandy Bottom, where all the workers, hot from their day in the fields, went for a cool plunge after work. They noticed that Velvet Pants never went with them.

"How does he keep so neat and clean?" they asked. It was Pete High who solved this mystery

"Yesterday morning," said Pete, "I woke up earlier than usual, and what do you suppose I see? Well, I hear a tap, tap, tap, like somebody was stealing downstairs on his tiptoes. I peek out o' the door, and it's Velvet Pants. Just for fun, I follow him. He goes down the creek where the water ain't more than ankle-deep. He takes a stick and goes like this, 'Ah, ah, ah,' and pokes at the bushes each time he says 'ah.' Then he gives one big loud 'Ahhhhhhh,' and lunges with his stick at the bushes; then he bows low, like he was an actor in a show. He takes a bath then, splashing a little water on himself like a cat does; but he doesn't go in above his ankles. I guess he's afraid of the water."

"Mebbe he ain't much on swimming," said one of the other hands, "but he sure can twang a mean guitar. He's giving Janey Crosby lessons."

Pete High scowled.

"He is, is he? First I heard about it."

"She likes him," teased the other man. "Says he's got such lovely manners; just like what you ain't, Pete."

"She don't know how yella he is," Pete High growled, "but she will."

On Saturday afternoons most of Crosby Corners—men, women, and children—come to Sandy Bottom, bringng bathing suits. It is not a very big pool; at its deepest part it is not much over six feet deep.

How it happened that the small man with the velvet trousers should be passing Sandy Bottom that Saturday noon at the moment when the freckled Johnny Nelson was floundering in the water does not matter. Why Johnny Nelson should be drowning at all is something of a puzzle, for he was the best swimmer in the county. It also happened that just as Johnny was going down for the ninth or tenth time, Janey Crosby and a party of girl friends came down to the pool.

They saw Velvet Pants trying to reach Johnny with a young tree wrenched from the bank. The small man was a picture of frantic helplessness.

"Save me, Velvet Pants! Save me!" bawled Johnny.

"Not know how," screamed Velvet Pants in agony.

Velvet Pants, finding that he could not reach Johnny with the tree, had fallen on his knees and was praying aloud in his own tongue. Then it also happened that Pete High came racing through the bushes.

"I'll save you, Johnny!" he cried dramatically. He plunged in and brought Johnny to the bank. The prayers of Velvet Pants became prayers of thanksgiving. Pete High stood regarding him with disgust.

"Oh, Velvet Pants," said Janey Crosby, "why didn't you jump in and save him?"

Slowly, sadly, the small man shrugged his shoulders.

"Not know water," he said, "not know sweem."

He said it very much as if he were stating a fact, the truth of which he regretted, but a fact nevertheless. He looked dismayed and surprised when Janey Crosby and the others turned away from him.

After that, Velvet Pants was an outcast. The men spoke to him only when it was necessary, and then briefly and even harshly. He did not seem to understand; he would try to tell them things, making many gestures; but he had not the words to make himself clear, nor had they the desire to listen to him.

End of Part 1

The Unfamiliar

Part 2
by Richard Connell

Toward the end of the harvest season, it was Janey Crosby's birthday. It was the most important social event of the year in Crosby Corners. All the village was invited, and all the village came—the women in their fresh skirts, the men soaped and collared and uncomfortable, but happy. They brought presents as if they were bringing a tribute to a queen, and Janey, as graciously as a reigning sovereign, took them all and smiled.

The party was an affair of considerable tone, with dancing, two helpings of ice cream all around, and a three-piece orchestra.

The dancing was half over. Janey and Pete High, her current partner, had gone out on the porch.

"Look!" exclaimed Pete. "What's that sitting down there?"

Janey made out a small, bent figure sitting, chin on hands, eyes turned toward the lighted hall.

"Why, it's Velvet Pants!"

"Shall I chase him away?" asked Pete, swelling out his chest. Janey laid a restraining hand on his arm.

"No. The poor fellow's probably lonesome. Everybody is here but him."

"He deserves to be lonesome," said Pete. "He's yella."

"Would you jump in to save a person from drowning if you didn't know how to swim?"

"Of course I would," replied Pete promptly. "Now, see here, Janey Crosby, don't you go sticking up for that chap. He's not fit to associate with men."

She sat gazing at the small, miserable figure; then she made a sudden resolution.

"I'm going to ask him to come up to the party," she said.

"No, you ain't."

"Whose birthday is this, Pete High? I guess it won't do any harm to give him a dish of ice cream. You don't have to associate with him. Run down and tell him I'd like to see him."

Pete mumbled protests, but he went. As Velvet Pants approached the porch, Janey Crosby saw that he was wearing a new, clean shirt, that his black locks had been parted and buttered, and that his shoes had been brightly shined.

"This is my birthday, Velvet Pants," said Janey. "I want you to help me celebrate it."

The small man seemed overcome; he bowed twice very low. Then he spoke. He spoke mechanically, as if the words had been often rehearsed.

"I had no gif' for you on your birthday, Mees Crosby, but I haf learn a song American to seeng for you. I hear heem on funnygraf. I hope you like."

He said it humbly, but not without a certain pride that attends the accomplishment of a difficult feat.

Janey laughed delightedly. "Wasn't that a sweet idea! Wait! I'll call the others; no, better still, you come into the hall and sing, so they can all hear."

Velvet Pants looked horrified at this suggestion.

"But, no," he protested. "I do not seeng good."

"That's all right. They won't know the difference," said Janey laughingly. "Come along."

She pushed him through the open doorway. The guests looked up. What would Janey Crosby do next?

"Folks," announced Janey Crosby, "Mr. Velvet Pants is going to sing for us. He learned a little American song just for my birthday. Wasn't that nice of him?"

It was evident from the face of Pete High, who stood in the doorway, that he did not think it was particularly nice.

The small, brown man glanced uncertainly about the hall; then he began to play chords upon his guitar. Some of the ladies giggled. In a round, clear tenor Velvet Pants began to sing:

"Kees me hagain, kees me hagain,
Kees me hagain, and hagain."

His memory seemed to go back on him at this point; he groped for a moment for the words. There was a slight ripple of applause that was checked suddenly. Pete High strode up to Velvet Pants and was facing him.

"Just a minute there," said Pete. "What do you mean by singing a song like that to Miss Crosby?"

The small man looked puzzled.

"It ees only song American I know," he said.

"Yeah? Well, I'm going to teach you to sing it out of the other side of your mouth. Come outside with me."

"Pete High," broke in Janey, "don't you go fighting with him. He didn't mean any harm; he probably doesn't know what the words mean."

"I told him never to say anything to you, whether he understood it or not," stormed Pete. "Come on, you."

Velvet Pants made an attempt to steal away, but Pete blocked his path.

"You're going out on the lawn with me," said Pete.

"And seeng?" asked the little man, who seemed somewhat dazed by what was happening.

"No, fight."

"Fight?"

"Yes, fight."

"But I do no hate you, Meester Pete."

"Well, I hate you. Come on."

"But how we fight?" inquired the small man; he was pale beneath his tan, and trembling. For an answer, Pete thrust a clenched fist under the man's nose. The man drew his head back and shivered.

"No!" he said, shaking his head. "No!"

"You won't fight?"

"No."

"You're a coward," declared Pete.

Velvet Pants shrugged his shoulders.

"Not know hand fights," he said.

Pete slapped him across the face with his open hand.

"Now will you fight?"

"Not know hand fights," said the man, drawing away. Pete, contempt on his face, gave him a push into the night. They heard the sound of feet on the path; Velvet Pants was running.

"Not know hand fights," Pete mimicked. "Did you ever in your life see such a rat?"

Next day, excitement swept Crosby Corners. Defender Monarch had gone crazy; and when that news spread, they forgot all about the conduct of Velvet Pants on the night before. As for him, he went about his work with a puzzled and hurt look on his face; he seemed still uncertain why the others did not respond to his smiles and attempts at friendliness.

Defender Monarch was the pride, and the terror, of the county. His owner, Ben Crosby, had raised him from a calf, wobbly on his legs, into a massive ton-and-a-half bull, with a chest like a haystack, a voice like thunder, and the temper of a demon. Ben Crosby had not dehorned him, because in cattle shows a good pair of horns is considered a point of merit in judging bulls, and the giant bull had won many blue ribbons. On this day Ben Crosby wished most earnestly that he had taken off those horns. A savage bull without horns is bad enough, but a savage bull with a pair of sharp, wicked horns is just about the most dangerous animal that walks.

Defender Monarch stood in his pasture, roaring a challenge to the world. By blind luck Ben Crosby was able to trick him into entering a big pen, but in the process Defender Monarch had given a sample of his viciousness by ripping Johnny Nelson's arm from elbow to shoulder and had failed by a hair's breadth to crush the life out of Ben Crosby himself. Once confined in the pen, Defender Monarch's rage knew no bounds. He hurled himself against the thick board sides so furiously that they creaked and trembled.

Luckily the pen was a stoutly built affair, perhaps fifty feet square. About it moved Defender Monarch, his small eyes blazing, alert. And perched on boxes and ladders, all of Crosby Corners, fascinated, watched.

"Isn't he just too terrible?" said Janey Crosby to Pete High.

"Oh, I don't know," answered Pete airily. "I've worked round him often."

"Not since he went crazy, Pete."

"No, mebbe not."

"See how he's looking right at us with those mean little eyes."

"I'm here," said Pete High reassuringly.

To get a better view, Janey Crosby climbed to the very top of the stepladder. There was a sharp crack as the top rail gave way, then horrified cries. She had fallen into the pen and lay unconscious almost at the feet of the mad bull.

The women screamed; the men ran about aimlessly, wildly, shouting orders at one another.

"Help! Janey's fallen into the pen."

"Get pitchforks!"

"Get a gun!"

"No use, we've only got bird shot."

"Someone will have to jump in."

"Where are you running to, Pete High?"

"To get a rope or something."

"You'll be too late."

Defender Monarch looked down at Janey and his eyes were evil. Then he looked at the ring of faces that lined the top of the pen. He seemed to understand the situation; he seemed to know that he had plenty of time, and he gloated. He turned away from Janey, trotted to the farther end of the pen, wheeled about, and surveyed the distance between himself and her body; then he lowered his head, with its gleaming prongs, and gathered his body for a charge.

The terrified onlookers became aware that something was in the pen besides Janey and the bull. A figure had come through the gate silently and swiftly. It was a small man in velvet trousers, and he was strolling toward Defender Monarch as casually and calmly as if the bull were a rosebush. Velvet Pants was a tiger, completely sure of himself. On his face there was not the slightest trace of fear. He was as matter-of-fact as if he were about to sit down to his breakfast. A cigarette hung limp from one corner of his lips. With the dainty strut they had noticed and made fun of, he walked slowly toward Defender Monarch. The animal, distracted, stood blinking at the little man. Within a few feet of the bull, Velvet Pants

halted; there was a flash of something red. It was Ben Crosby's red-flannel shirt that a few moments before had been drying on the line. The small man had waved it across the bull's face. Defender Monarch forgot Janey. He saw red, and he plunged toward it. The women turned their heads away; the men clenched their teeth. They saw

Velvet Pants slip aside with the quickness of a jungle cat and the bull, unable to check himself, jolt his head against one of the sides of the pen. Velvet Pants turned round, smiled pleasantly, and bowed very low to the spectators. They saw that he had in his right hand something long and bright that caught the rays of the sun; they realized that it was Grandpa Crosby's old Civil War sword that had hung in the dining room. He was holding it as lightly and easily as if it were a butter knife.

Defender Monarch, recovering from his fruitless charge against the wall, spun about; the red shirt was skillfully flapped before his bright, mad eyes. Once more, with a roar of wrath, he launched his bulk straight at Velvet Pants. Then something happened to Defender Monarch. It happened with such speed that all the onlookers saw was a flash; then the huge frame of the bull crumpled and sank down. Sticking from his left shoulder was the hilt of Grandpa Crosby's sword; the spectators saw the hilt only, for Velvet Pants had driven the point into Defender Monarch's heart.

The people of Crosby Corners say that Ben Crosby kissed the little tanned man on both cheeks, but this he denies; he admits, however, that he hugged him and patted him and said many words of gratitude and admiration to Velvet Pants, who seemed unable to understand why everyone was making so much of a fuss about him.

"And I called you a coward," Ben Crosby kept saying. "I called you a coward, and you went in and faced a mad bull without batting an eyelash."

"It was nuzzing," murmured the small brown man.

"Nothing to face a mad bull?"

Velvet Pants shrugged his shoulders.

"But I am bullfighter," he said. "In my country, Andalusia, I keel one, two, t'ree bull every Sunday for fun. Why should I fear bulls? I know bulls."

Other People Are Her Business

by Arnold Abrams

It had been a hard day, one made even harder because she was hobbling on crutches after a skiing accident, and Sharon McGrory-Buckley was feeling depressed when she met a longtime acquaintance near her office in North Shore University Hospital on Long Island.

"How are you?" he asked.

"Terrible," she replied. "These crutches can really get you down."

Her response was casual, made without much thought. His was not.

"What do you think you're talking about?" snapped her friend, a lifelong paraplegic, whose paralyzed legs confined him to a wheelchair. "Where do *you* come off feeling down? You don't know what it means."

Buckley still shakes her head when recalling the exchange. "It was a turning point in my life," she says. "It really made me think."

That incident, which took place several years ago, was particularly moving because making people think is Buckley's job. She is a medical social worker who, for the past decade, has helped thousands of North Shore patients cope with severe medical problems.

"I don't cure them, and I can't eliminate their pain," said Buckley, 33, who keeps a crutch in her office as a constant reminder of the hallway encounter. "But I can help patients handle such things, and I can provide options that might restore some normalcy to their lives."

Buckley must fill a wide variety of roles, including psychological counselor, patient advocate, researcher, and detective. In the course of any day, her duties might involve everything from counseling a heart patient about surgery or preparing a cancer victim for death to phoning patients' relatives, arranging nursing home admissions, setting up home-care schedules, or preparing insurance applications.

The means can be enormously complex, but her professional goals are relatively simple. "I am here to assist patients and their families in coping with illness and its problems," Buckley said. "A key part of that is hooking them up with appropriate resources—state agencies, county services, private care, or even family friends."

That is what social work is about. It is practiced across the country by more than 200,000 professionals, who, like teachers, do important work but receive relatively little pay or public appreciation.

"A social worker is someone who must deal with the system and make it work for the people who need it most," said Mary Brett, North Shore's associate director of social work, who supervises Buckley and her 53 coworkers. "Some people can spend a lifetime at that without really succeeding."

Buckley succeeds, according to her supervisor, through a combination of personal decency and professional drive. "Nobody cares more about the people who need her," Brett said, "and nobody is better at bringing resources to bear."

Most in need of Buckley's services are the elderly, whose advanced age, mental condition, and social situation often combine to render them sick, confused, and alone. Typical is the case of Mr. B, a long-time widower who, in his late 70s and living alone, checked into the hospital several months ago for treatment of severe back pains.

A once-vigorous man who took special pride in his independence and ability to live alone, Mr. B turned out to be a medical casebook. He had Parkinson's disease (a nerve disorder) as well as a variety of other problems.

Although his ailments were not life-threatening, the patient, frightened and uncertain about his future, went into deep depression. "You don't know what it feels like to lose control of your life," he told a recent visitor. "It was like I was a piece of luggage being bounced around by a bunch of strangers."

Mr. B gradually regained his strength and, with Buckley's help, a greater degree of control. But with those improvements came additional problems: his upcoming discharge from North Shore and the question of where to go.

His first choice was the studio apartment he had maintained since his wife's death some 20 years ago; his second was the home of a daughter. His last was a nursing home.

In helping Mr. B make a choice, Buckley determined that his shaky health would prevent him from living alone; that his daughter did not want to take him in; and that he would be terribly unhappy—enough to suffer potentially serious psychological consequences—in a nursing home.

"He says 'home' and I say 'good,'" Buckley said last week as Mr. B prepared to leave. "But the point is to keep him out of the hospital, and if we send him home alone in his condition, this man is likely to be back here before long."

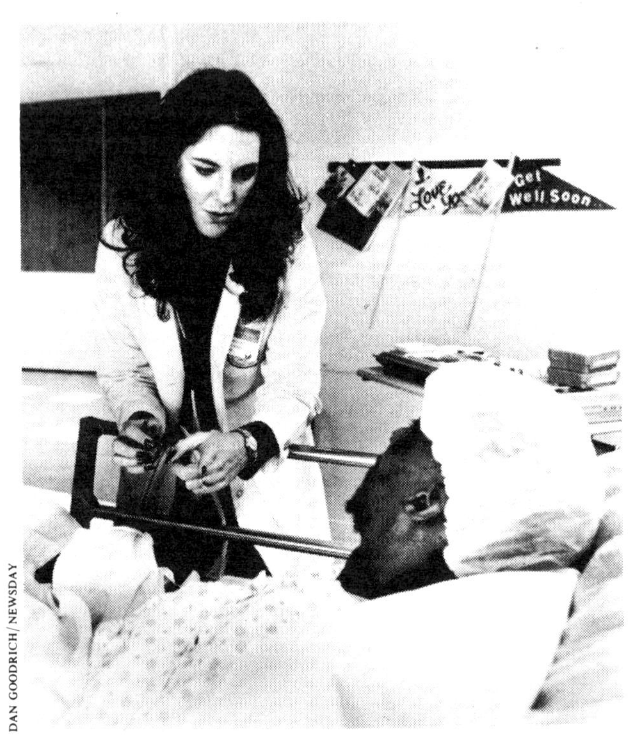

DAN GOODRICH/NEWSDAY

So the social worker came up with a compromise: The patient would go home, but would not live alone. After determining his insurance benefits, financial resources, and Medicaid eligibility, Buckley devised a medical-care program that included a 24-hour aide to provide basic housekeeping and physical care; a visiting nurse to monitor his condition; and help from Nassau County's Adult Protective Service, which aids individuals who lack family support.

"There's not going to be a happy ending to this story," the social worker confided. "But I take great comfort in the fact that I helped this man handle his immediate problems and, by providing options he could not have found on his own, possibly allowed him to enjoy a few more years before the situation turns. That may not seem like much, but it means a lot to me—and everything to him."

Buckley first learned about Mr. B in a cramped conference room, where she meets regularly with a hospital group that includes a head nurse and various professionals concerned with home care, post-hospital placement, and facility utilization. Each meeting involves careful study of patient lists and lengthy discussion of each person's medical problems and personal circumstances.

Armed with updated information, Buckley proceeds on her rounds, visiting each patient on her list—her average caseload is 15 to 20—and making firsthand inquiries about medical progress and private needs.

"Social work is one of the few disciplines in a hospital that deals with the patient as a whole," she remarked in the course of those rounds. "We deal with physical, psychological, and social needs. Almost everyone else has a much narrower focus."

When she introduced herself to Mitchell, for example, her presence prompted a visible sense of relief. Still recovering from serious head wounds suffered in a knife attack several days earlier, he had difficulty discussing the incident—which was nearly fatal—and was concerned about an approaching interview with a member of the district attorney's office.

"I still have trouble talking about this," he said. "I don't think I'm ready to talk to a DA about it."

"Then you probably don't have to," Buckley replied. "I'll look into it and let you know. But, if time is that essential, the least we can do is make sure some friends are with you when you're talking. Make up a list, and I'll help round them up.''

She also will help him obtain state victim's aid assistance, fill out insurance forms, arrange physical and occupational therapy, and, finally, work out a hospital discharge plan that will allow him to resume a normal life with minimal stress.

Mitchell, a Vietnam veteran who is in his mid-30s and has had employment problems, was not used to someone showing such concern about his welfare. ''Thank you so much,'' he said as Buckley left. ''You know, nobody else has asked me about all these things. I really appreciate it.''

But things do not always run so smoothly for Buckley, a native Long Islander who attended Hofstra and first came to North Shore as a graduate student in social work at Adelphi.

All too often, she said, she must watch helplessly while someone who entered the hospital in reasonable health starts to weaken as a terrible disease takes hold. ''It is so hard to watch that happen,'' she added, ''and it never stops hurting.''

She works hard, however, to keep the hurt from showing. ''It's not that we are cold,'' she said of herself and other medical social workers. ''We are trained copers. We have to cope. If we can't, we don't belong. And coping leaves little room for tears.''

But the tears still come—in private—for patients like one young woman who entered the hospital ten years ago, shortly after Buckley had started working there.

Like Buckley, she was 23 and was studying for her master's degree. She also bore a striking physical resemblance to the social worker: tall, with long dark hair and blue eyes. She had melanoma, a form of skin cancer than can spread throughout the body.

"It was terrible," Buckley recalled. "She was my double, and I had to go through the process of watching her die. It is an awesome thing, having to face your own death at age 23, but it marked my start as a social worker. If you have to counsel patients about their death, first you must face your own."

Now she is helping Stanley to face his. He is an intelligent man who used to play with strength and grace on local tennis courts and enjoyed walking with his wife through wooded areas bordering Long Island Sound.

Physically active, loving the outdoors, he retired from his high school teaching position several years ago, at the relatively early age of 59, in order to fully enjoy his retirement years.

Which he did with great pleasure until one day last summer, when he went out on the tennis court and, slightly bothered by a mild headache, experienced something he had never encountered before.

"I just couldn't do anything out there," he said. "I would swing at the ball and miss, and when I tried to run it was like moving in slow motion. My partners asked what was the matter, and I couldn't tell them. Everything just was wrong."

Stanley blocked the tennis disaster from his mind, but in the following days other ordinary things began going wrong: He had difficulty seating himself, stepping into pants, tying his shoelaces, driving his car.

It all happened within one week. And when Stanley finally went for a medical examination, doctors discovered a walnut-sized growth on his brain. He would never be the same.

"The worst part is the disabling effect," he said of the operation that removed the growth but left him largely bedridden. "It takes you from a a normal life to a child-like existence. It is very discouraging."

Deeply moved by the plight of this once-vigorous man, Buckley drew up an intensive recovery program for his lengthy hospital stay. It combined psychological counseling with physical and occupational therapy, and it has continued as part of home-care treatment she also arranged.

But the results of such efforts are limited. Hours and hours of therapy have given Stanley the phsyical capability of a small child. Prospects of substantial recovery are slim.

The cancer victim expressed deep gratitude to Buckley, during a visit she made to his home last week, for the direction, encouragement, and courage she had given him and his wife during their long siege. But he also acknowledged the possibility of dying.

"The disablement is far worse than the prospect of death," he said without a trace of self-pity. "In fact, if I should worsen, I think I would welcome an end to everything."

Afterward, returning to the hospital, Buckley was asked how, in light of Stanley's future prospects, she bears the pain of so many cases like his.

She frowned at the question—an answer in itself—and then said: "I concentrate on the physical and psychological progress he and his wife have made. I don't want to project ahead. I find it doesn't pay."

descent into the maelstrom[1]

by Edgar Allan Poe

"About three years ago," said my guide, "something happened to me that has never before happened to mortal man. At least no man has ever lived to tell about it. The six hours of deadly terror which I endured have broken me up body and soul. You suppose me a very old man—but I'm not. It took less than a single day to change my hair from jet black to white. Now my hands shake and my nerves are shot." He went on: "I have brought you to this spot overlooking the ocean so that you could hear the whole story with the exact location right before your eyes."

We had been at the top of the mountain for about ten minutes. I perceived that a strong current was developing in the ocean beneath us. Even while I watched, this current acquired a monstrous velocity. In five minutes the whole sea was whipped into a fury. The water burst into frenzied activity—heaving, boiling, hissing—rotating in many gigantic circles, all whirling and plunging with a speed which water never assumes, except in waterfalls.

In a few minutes more, the surface of the water became smoother and the whirlpools, one by one, disappeared. Huge streaks of foam appeared where none had been seen

[1]Maelstrom: A powerful, often violent, whirlpool that sucks in objects within a given radius.

before. These streaks came together in a spiraling motion, and started to form a whirling mass of water more vast than any one of those which had faded away.

Suddenly—very suddenly—this whirlpool assumed a distinct and definite existence, in a circle of more than a mile in diameter. At the edge of the whirl was a broad belt of gleaming spray. The interior, as far as the eye could fathom it, was a smooth, shining, and jet-black wall of water, speeding dizzily round and round.

The mountain trembled to its very base, and the rock rocked. I threw myself upon my face, and clung to the scant grass.

"This," I said at length to the old man, "must be the great whirlpool of the Maelstrom."

"You have had a good look at the whirlpool now," said the old man. "If you will creep round this crag, to deaden the roar of the water, I will tell you a story that will convince you I ought to know something of the Maelstrom.

"It was almost three years ago today that this episode took place. On the tenth day of July, 18—, there blew the most terrible hurricane that ever came out of the heavens. And yet for most of the day there was only a gentle breeze from the southwest. The sun shone brightly, so that the oldest seaman among us could not have predicted what was to follow.

"The three of us—my two brothers and myself—had crossed over to the islands about two o'clock p.m., and soon nearly loaded the boat with fish. It was just seven o'clock when we weighed our catch and started for home. We wanted to cross the channel at slack water, which is when the water is between tides and is neither flowing in nor flowing out. We knew that would be at eight o'clock.

"In the meantime the breeze stopped blowing and we were becalmed. But in less than a minute the storm was upon us—in less than two the sky was entirely overcast. What with the black sky and the driving spray, it became suddenly so dark that we could not see each other in the boat.

"I can't begin to describe the hurricane that started to blow. The oldest seaman never experienced anything like it. The hurricane was a cruel master; at its first puff, both our masts went overboard. My younger brother, lashed to it for safety, went overboard with the mainmast. How my older brother escaped I cannot say. I threw myself flat on the deck, and with my hands grasping a ring-bolt near the foot of the mast, I held on for dear life.

"For some moments we were completely deluged. I held my breath and clung to the bolt. When finally I could stand it no longer and had to take a breath, I raised myself upon my knees and got my head above water. I was trying to collect my senses when I felt somebody grasp my arm. It was my older brother, and my heart leaped for joy, for I had been sure that he was overboard. But the next moment all this joy was turned into horror—for he put his mouth close to my ear, and screamed out the word 'Maelstrom!'

"That one word threw me into a violent fit. I knew that with the wind that now drove us on, we were bound for the whirlpool of the Maelstrom, and nothing could save us!

"Shortly, the waves disappeared and we were enveloped in foam. The boat made a sharp half turn to the left, and then shot off in its new direction like a thunderbolt. We were now in the belt of surf that always surrounds the whirl; and I thought that in another moment we would plunge into its very center.

"It may seem strange, but now, when we were in the very jaws of the gulf, I felt more composed than when we were only approaching it. Having given up hope, I got rid of that terror which unmanned me at first. I supposed it was despair that deadened my nerves.

"How often we made the circuit of the belt it is impossible to say. We careened round and round for perhaps an hour, moving gradually into the middle of the surge. All this time I had never let go of the ring-bolt. My brother was at the back of the boat, holding on to a small, empty water cask that had been securely lashed down.

"As we approached the brink of the pit, he let go his hold upon the water cask, and tried to force my hands from the ring-bolt, as it could not afford us both a secure grasp. I never felt deeper grief than when I saw him attempt this act—although I knew he was a madman when he did it—a raving maniac through sheer fright. I did not care, however, to contest the point with him. I knew it could make no difference, so I let him have the bolt, and went back to the cask. Scarcely had I secured myself in my new position, when we gave a wild lurch to the right, and rushed headlong into the pit. I thought it was all over.

"As I felt the sickening sweep of the descent, I had instinctively tightened my hold upon the barrel, and closed my eyes. For some seconds I dared not open them. I expected instant destruction, and wondered why I was not already in my death struggles with the water. But moment after moment elapsed. I still lived. I took courage, opened my eyes, and looked once again upon the scene.

"Never shall I forget the sensation of awe, horror, and admiration with which I gazed about me. The boat appeared to be hanging, as if by magic, midway down, upon the interior surface of the vast and spiraling funnel. Round and round we swept—not with any uniform movement—but in dizzying swings and jerks, that sent us sometimes only a few hundred yards—sometimes nearly the complete circuit of the whirl. Our progress downward, at each revolution, was slow, but very noticeable. Both above and below us were fragments of vessels, lumber, tree trunks, and many smaller articles, such as pieces of house furniture, broken boxes, and barrels.

"I now began to watch, with a strange interest, the numerous things that floated around us. I must have been delirious, for I even sought amusement in speculating on who would win the race to the pit below. At length, after making several guesses, and being wrong each time—this fact—the fact of my constant miscalculation, gave me an idea that made my limbs tremble and my heart pound.

"It was not a new terror that affected me, but the dawn of an exciting hope. This hope arose from memory, and partly from present observation. I called to mind the great variety of debris that lined the coast, having been absorbed and then thrown forth by the whirlpool. Most of the articles were shattered in an extraordinary way. They were totally rough and splintered. But some of them were not marred at all. I could not account for this difference except by supposing that the roughened fragments were the only ones which had been completely absorbed—that the others had entered the whirl at so late a period of the tide, or, for some reason, had descended so slowly after entering, that they did not reach the bottom before the turn of the tide. It was possible that they might be whirled up again to the top, without undergoing the fate of those which had been drawn in earlier or absorbed more rapidly.

"I always made two important observations. The first was that, as a general rule, the larger the bodies were, the more rapid their descent. The second, that, between two masses of equal size, the one cylindrical and the other of any other shape, the cylinder was absorbed more slowly.

"I no longer hesitated what to do. I made up my mind to tie myself to the water cask, to cut it loose from the boat, and to throw myself with it into the water. I attracted my brother's attention by signs, and tried to make him understand what I was about to do. He only shook his head despairingly, and refused to move from his station by the ring-bolt. It was impossible to reach him. The nature of the emergency gave me no time; and so, with a

bitter struggle, I resigned him to his fate. I fastened myself to the cask with ropes and threw myself with it into the sea.

"The result was precisely what I had hoped it might be. Since I'm the one who is telling you this tale, you see that I did escape. As you already know all the details, I will bring my story quickly to conclusion. It might have been an hour, or thereabout, after I jumped out of the boat, that it swirled far below me. It made three or four wild turns, and taking my brother with it, plunged headlong into the gulf below.

"The barrel to which I was attached sank only a little farther, when a great change took place in the whirlpool. The slope of the sides of the vast funnel became less and less steep. The turns of the whirl grew, gradually, less and less violent. The whirlpool started slowly to fill with water and the gulf disappeared.

"The sky was clear and the full moon was setting, when I found myself on the surface of the ocean in full view of the shoreline. I was directly above the spot where the whirlpool had been. It was the slack tide, but the sea still heaved in mountainous waves from the effects of the hurricane. I was borne violently into the channel, and in a few minutes, was hurried down the coast into the fishing grounds.

"A boat picked me up. I was speechless from the memory of the horror I'd been through. Those who drew me on board were my old mates, but they knew me no more than they would have known a traveler from another land. My hair, which had been raven black the day before, was as white as you see it now. Even my face had changed. I told them my story—they did not believe it. I now tell it to you—and I can scarcely expect you to put more faith in it than did those fishermen."

Exploring the Amazon

by Paula DiPerna

When I arrived in Manaus, a city in the middle of the Amazon jungle of Brazil, it was December and 2:00 a.m., but the summer air was as hot and smelly as a woolen blanket left out in the rain. As I rode into town, my taxi driver told me that spare auto parts were hard to get; I believed him. The taxi sounded as though it once had been a washing machine.

It was my first taste of life in the Amazon. I was the "advance man," if you will, for Jacques Cousteau's recent Amazon expedition. Cousteau, his son Jean-Michel, and their camera and science teams were to explore the Amazon River from its source in the Andes to the place where it emptied into the Atlantic in order to film several television documentaries. I would look for filmable stories—underwater gold mining, giant dams, fish migrations, for example. When the famous ship *Calypso* came into a river port, I'd meet her and supply my notes on the region she was about to enter. Or I'd fly ahead of a truck expedition to collect names of contacts the crew would need. I also would help coordinate the operation of sending equipment and people to remote locations within an undeveloped area as large as the continental United States.

The Cousteau plan was complicated. With *Calypso*, a seaplane, a helicopter, an Amazon-style riverboat called the *Anaconda* for penetrating shallow streams, other types of craft, diving and camera crews, and scientists, the Cousteaus intended to study the Amazon River and its tributaries—the rivers and streams that feed into it, both above and below water—and also to explore the deep forest. They would film their adventures as well as reveal the intricate beauty of the largest tropical rain forest left on earth. Their work also would examine the destruction caused by development in the Amazon region.

Manaus was the starting point. It is a major Brazilian city on the Rio Negro, the biggest tributary of the Amazon River proper. Manaus also is the site of Brazil's National Amazon Research Institute (INPA), where I could interview leading Brazilian scientists.

From my hotel-room balcony, I could see the river easily. There were some big cargo ships but many more small canoes loaded so low in the water that all you could see were piles of bananas and other freight. The Rio Negro is only one of the thousand great and small rivers that lace the forest and can rise a dozen feet with the rainy season and then fall away drastically. The river people—called *caboclos*—depend on the rivers to get around.

The rain forest itself is a beautiful, tangled green web of trees, trees, trees, as far as the eye can take it in from a plane or from land. Little light penetrates, but a rainstorm can make the most densely packed trees shudder. The rainy season was just beginning in Manaus.

It was here that I learned the adventure of telephoning in the Amazon. I since have calculated that in the course of my Amazon stay I placed some 4000 phone calls, about half of which did not go through on the first attempt. Where there were phone lines, rain soaked them; where there was a radio patch operator, I'd be forgotten. Sometimes there'd be a busy signal on the line before I even dialed a number. Frequently, a clear conversation would fade midsentence, and I eventually imagined a giant mouth in the sky gobbling my conversation just to drive me crazy. But on the first day, these fantasies had not yet taken hold, and when I finally got through to INPA they were expecting me.

INPA's buildings are wedged among rain forest on the outskirts of Manaus. Blue butterflies and lively lizards dart across the paths. Much of the INPA research interested me. For example, what happens to fish species that live on fruit and seeds falling in the rivers when those fruits trees are cut down? Filming the feeding and the cutting would be important, and I needed to know when it happened and where. This was typical of the hundreds of questions that came up during the project. At this first meeting, I talked awhile with the INPA director and saw about half a dozen other INPA people—a record for a single day in the laid-back Amazon.

Several days later, I flew to Brasilia to meet the Cousteaus and Celso Luiz de Oliveira, their friend who had arranged the meetings necessary to obtain formal expedition permission from many government departments. During the meetings in Brasilia, I gathered names and phone numbers of officials whom we turned to later for help. I'd call, for example, to liberate film equipment from stubborn customs inspectors, or to arrange an airforce lift for one of our trucks that had been marooned at the wrong end of the continent because the barge that was supposed to transport it never arrived.

After a productive few days in Brasilia, the Cousteaus left to prepare *Calypso*'s departure from the United States and I returned to Manaus to set up an expedition office and base there. I would be on my own for the next few months.

I worked out of the Hotel Monaco in Manaus and traveled to promising film sites, led by my library research, the Cousteau's suggestions, an interview, a news clip, hearsay, or my own instincts. Sometimes I'd be gone from Manaus overnight, sometimes for a few weeks. I had complete independence, and reported either by telephone or telex to the New York office or directly to the Cousteaus.

A typical "to do" list for a day in the office might include: study some Portuguese, which I was learning by doing; read Henry Bates (a 19th-century naturalist) on leaf-cutter ants; organize files on Amazon development projects; investigate costs of jeep insurance; find a cook for the *Anaconda*; write up notes from an interview with a crocodile specialist; locate dry ice for storing fish tissue samples. An office day also would include routine work such as picking up my airline tickets or office supplies, and endless telephoning (and nontelephoning).

There was no such thing as a typical day in the bush, although I planned my travels along the route the film teams later would follow. Sometimes I'd walk in a jungle area with a local guide, and every now and then an animal—a monkey or a bird—would take off, setting the trees in motion as it went. Some days, there was a lingering absence of sound in the daytime, except the crunching of one's footsteps on leaves or fallen branches, but night brought an orchestra of calls and answers, chirps and scraping noises. Once, in Leticia, Colombia, I heard what

PHOTO COURTESY OF THE COUSTEAU SOCIETY, INC., 930 WEST 21ST STREET, NORFOLK, VA 23517, A MEMBERSHIP SUPPORTED ENVIRONMENTAL ORGANIZATION.

sounded like a flute being played beside a stream running over rocks. It was the *oropendola*, a bird whose call mimics falling water. It is one of the loveliest sounds I know.

Most people ask me about Amazon dangers—poisonous snakes waiting to strike, killer fish ready to chomp off fingers that linger in a stream, bats ready to swoop. Any of these things could happen at any time, but usually they don't. One person in the middle of the Amazon is like one person in the middle of the United States, and I felt protected by the odds.

I was not immune to the insects, though. The Amazon belongs to them. There are huge cockroaches everywhere, and they get inside any suitcase. At night, if I had to read by flashlight, tiny moths would hover in the beam. But most nerve-racking were the mosquitos. No spray, no lotion, can protect against their diving in your ears. As

you try to sleep, they whine through the sheets you pull over your head, even through blankets.

Although I doubt my life was ever truly in danger, once I may have taken a foolish chance by mixing with what I later learned was pretty tough company. I had arrived by pickup truck, loaned to me by the farm-reform agency, at an outpost near Bolivia.

There, men dove from platforms anchored in the middle of the muddy Madeira River, another tributary, holding huge tubes that sucked up the river bottom so that it could be panned for gold. The water looked like chocolate milk, and the current was treacherous. No underwater visibility, I noted, but a fascinating scene: miners sleep in hammocks under trees along the riverbanks; malaria is rampant; and there are no garbage cans, just clearings in the forest.

I needed to see the diving operation up close to be able to describe what could be filmed, so I called out to a miner and asked him to ferry me, for a price if need be. My driver looked worried, but I chalked it up to excessive male protectiveness, and besides, I didn't want to pay to bring him, too. I jumped into the canoe and sailed out. The miners were pleasant enough, and I interviewed them on the barges about how much gold they get in a day and how long they can stay underwater, breathing through air hoses. I watched them work. Only when I was back in the pickup truck did my driver tell me that some of the miners I'd been chatting with were murderers who cut the air hoses of other miners they did not like.

One of my most notable experiences occurred when I went on the *Anaconda* with a film crew and two INPA biologists to film a seasonal fish migration. Hundreds of fish, so dense they look like a shadow on the river surface, swim along the bank. But the Amazonian river dolphins[1] also follow the fish to eat them and frequently get caught in fishermen's nets. Caboclos believe the river dolphins magically can take human form. In the Amazon, instead of slaughtering trapped dolphins (as happens in Japan), people save them.

We sailed to Praia Grande, a white sand beach on the Rio Negro, and waited. One day, two days, no fish, no dolphins. For me, the waiting was a gift of time—no telephone, no telex, no errands. I read and rewrote my notes.

On the third day, the sun burned down and there was no breeze. The waters of the Rio Negro are black because of acid from decaying vegetation; they are so dark that,

[1]Dolphins: Members of a variety of small-toothed whales.

as I swam, I could not see the hand I threw ahead of me. Still, I swam, for it was the only heat relief. Then the fishermen yelled, "Dolphins!" Two were trapped and we ran back to the beach, film equipment hastily collected.

The fishermen were already closing in on their catch. Fish flapped, a hundred tailfins seeking escape. But the glistening dolphins held my eyes. They were beached as the nets were pulled to shore. The fishermen caressed the animals and poured water onto their backs so they wouldn't overheat. The biologists quickly measured the dolphins and took blood samples. I stroked the dolphins with my fingertips. Their skin was like warm ice melting, as pleasurable a touch as I have ever experienced. Then the animals were released. They swam in what seemed like a triumphant circle and were gone with the last light of day.

Unique moments like this made me wonder whether I wanted to leave the Amazon. I finally did after 11 months, in November 1982. The Cousteaus and their teams were still at work there, but it felt like time to take up New York life again. I left as I had arrived, through Manaus on a sleek jet that carried me in a few hours from the heart of the Amazon to New York City. It was hard to believe that I had so recently been where rain on the roof (when there is one) sounds like a thousand nails being hammered, where birds can mimic the sound of falling water, where people respect dolphins and help them swim away.

The Californian's Tale

by Mark Twain

Thirty-five years ago I was out prospecting on the Stanislaus, tramping all day long with pick and pan and horn, and washing a hatful of dirt here and there, always expecting to make a rich strike, and never doing it.

It was a lonesome land! Not a sound in all those peaceful stretches of grass and woods but the drowsy hum of insects; no glimpse of man or beast; nothing to keep up your spirits and make you glad to be alive. And so at last, in the early part of the afternoon, when I caught sight of a human creature, I felt a most grateful uplift. This person was a man about forty-five years old, and he was standing at the gate of a cozy little rose-clad cottage. It had the look of being lived in and petted and cared for and looked after; and so had its front yard, which was a garden of flowers, abundant and flourishing. I was invited in, of course, and required to make myself at home—it was the custom of the country.

It was delightful to be in such a place, after long weeks of daily and nightly familiarity with miners' cabins. I could not have believed that a rag carpet could feast me so, and so content me; or that there could be such comfort to the soul in wallpaper and framed pictures; and bright-colored tidies and lamp-mats; and Windsor chairs; and varnished what-nots, with seashells and books and china vases on them; and the score of little unclassifiable tricks and touches that a woman's hand distributes about a home. The delight that was in my heart showed in my face, and the man saw it and was pleased; saw it so plainly that he answered it as if it had been spoken.

"All her work," he said, caressingly; "she did it all herself—every bit." And he took the room in with a glance that was full of affectionate worship.

He took me into a bedroom so that I might wash my hands; such a bedroom as I had not seen for years: white counterpane, white pillows, carpeted floor, papered walls, pictures, dressing table, with mirror and pincushion and dainty toilet things; and in the corner a washstand, with real chinaware bowl and pitcher, and with soap in a china dish, and on a rack more than a dozen towels—towels too clean and white for one out of practice to use without some vague sense of misdoing. So my face spoke again, and he answered with grateful words:

"All her work; she didt it all herself—every bit. Nothing here that hasn't felt the touch of her hand. Now you would think—but I mustn't talk so much."

By this time I was wiping my hands and glancing from detail to detail of the room's belongings, as one is apt to do when he is in a new place, where everything he sees is a comfort to his eye and his spirit. I became conscious, in one of those unaccountable ways, you know, that there was something there somewhere that the man wanted me to discover for myself. I looked around the room slowly and carefully. At last I knew I must be looking straight at the thing—knew it from the pleasure issuing in invisible waves from him. He broke into a happy laugh and rubbed his hands together, and cried out: "That's it! You've found it. I knew you would. It's her picture."

I went to the little black-walnut bracket on the farther wall. It contained the sweetest girlish face, and the most beautiful, as it seemed to me, that I had ever seen. The man drank the admiration from my face and was fully satisfied.

"Nineteen her last birthday," he said, as he put the picture back, "and that was the day we were married. When you see her—ah, just wait till you see her!"

"Where is she? When will she be in?"

"Oh, she's away now. She's gone to see her people. They live forty or fifty miles from here. She's been gone two weeks today."

"When do you expect her back?"

"This is Wednesday. She'll be back Saturday, in the evening—about nine o'clock, likely."

I felt a sharp sense of disappointment.

"I'm sorry, because I'll be gone then," I said, regretfully.

"Gone? No—why should you go? Don't go. She'll be so disappointed.

"You see, she likes to have people come and stop with us—people who know things, and can talk—people like you. She delights in it; for she knows—oh, she knows nearly everything herself, and can talk, oh, like a bird—and the books she reads, why, you would be astonished. Don't go; it's only a little while, you know, and she'll be so disappointed.

"There, now tell her to her face you could have stayed to see her, and you wouldn't."

That second glimpse broke down my good resolution. I would stay. Toward twilight on Thursday a big miner from three miles away came—one of the grizzled, stranded pioneers—and gave us a warm greeting, clothed in grave and sober speech. Then he said: "I only just dropped over to ask about the little madam and to see when she's coming home. Any news from her?"

"Oh yes, a letter. Would you like to hear it, Tom?"

"Well, I should think I would, if you don't mind, Henry!"

Henry got the letter out of his wallet; it was a charming and gracious piece of writing with a postscript full of affectionate regards and messages to Tom and Joe and Charley and other close friends and neighbors.

As the reader finished, he glanced at Tom and cried out: "Oho, you're at it again! Take your hands away, and let me see your eyes. You always do that when I read a letter from her, I will write and tell her."

"Oh no, you mustn't, Henry. I'm getting old, you know, and any little disappointment makes me want to cry. I thought she'd be here herself, and now you've got only a letter."

"Well, now, what put that in your head? I thought everybody knew she wasn't coming till Saturday."

"Saturday! Why, come to think, I did know it. I wonder what's the matter with me lately? Certainly I knew it. Ain't we all getting ready for her? Well, I must be going now. But I'll be on hand when she comes, old man!"

Late Friday afternoon another gray veteran tramped over from his cabin a mile or so away and said the boys wanted to have a little gaiety and a good time Saturday night, if Henry thought she wouldn't be too tired after her journey to be kept up.

"Tired? She tired! Oh, hear the man! Joe, *you* know she'd sit up six weeks to please any one of you!"

When Joe heard that there was a letter, he asked to have it read, and the loving messages in it for him broke the old fellow all up; but he said he was such an old wreck that that would happen to him if she only just mentioned his name. "Lord, we miss her so!" he said.

Saturday afternoon I found I was taking out my watch pretty often. Henry noticed it and began to show uneasiness. Several times he said: "I'm getting worried, I'm getting right down worried. I know she's not due till about nine o'clock, and yet something seems to be trying to warn me that something's happened. You don't think anything has happened, do you?"

I was glad when Charley, another veteran, arrived toward the edge of the evening and did his best to drive away his friend's apprehensions.

"Anything *happened* to her? Henry, that's pure nonsense. There isn't anything going to happen to her; just make your mind easy as to that. What did the letter say? Said she was well, didn't it? And said she'd be here by nine o'clock, didn't it? She'll be here, as sure as you are born."

Pretty soon Tom and Joe arrived, and then all hands set about adorning the house with flowers. Toward nine the three miners said that as they had brought their instruments they might as well tune up, for the boys and girls would soon be arriving now, and hungry for a good, old-fashioned breakdown. The trio took their places side by side and began to play some rattling dance music. Their instruments danced with the eager anticipation of the lady's return.

It was getting very close to nine. Henry was standing in the door with his eyes directed up the road, his body swaying to the torture of his mental distress. He had been made to drink to his wife's health and safety several times, and now Tom shouted: "All hands stand by! One more drink, and she's here!"

Joe brought the glasses on a waiter and served the party. I reached for one of the two remaining glasses, but

Joe growled, under his breath: "Drop that! Take the other."

Which I did, Henry was served last. He had hardly swallowed his drink when the clock began to strike. He listened till it finished, his face growing pale and paler. Then he said: "Boys, I'm sick with fear. Help me—I want to lie down!"

They helped him to the sofa. He began to nestle and drowse, but presently spoke like one talking in his sleep, and said: "Did I hear horses' feet? Have they come?"

One of the veterans answered, close to his ear: "It was Jimmy Parrish come to say the party got delayed, but they're right up the road a piece and coming along. Her horse is lame, but she'll be here in half an hour."

"Oh, I'm so thankful nothing has happened!"

He was asleep almost before the words were out of his mouth. In a moment those handy men had his clothes off and had tucked him into his bed in the chamber where I had washed my hands. They closed the door and came back. Then they seemed to be preparing to leave, but I said: "Please don't go, gentlemen. She won't know me; I am a stranger."

They glanced at each other. Then Joe said: "She? Poor thing, she's been dead nineteen years!"

"Dead?"

"That or worse. She went to see her folks half a year after she was married, and on her way back, on a Saturday evening, the Indians captured her within five miles of this place,and she's never been heard of since."

"And he lost his mind in consequence?"

"Never has been sane an hour since. But he only gets bad when this time of the year comes around. Then we begin to drop in here, three days before she's due, to encourage him up and ask if he's heard from her, and

Saturday we all come and fix up the house with flowers, and get everything ready for a dance. We've done it every year for nineteen years. The first Saturday there was twenty-seven of us, without counting the women; there's only three of us now, and the women are all gone. We

drug him to sleep, or he would go wild; then he's all right for another year—thinks she's with him till the last three or four days come round; then he begins to look for her and gets out his poor old letter, and we come and ask him to read it to us. Lord, she was a darling!"

from Always Running

by Luis J. Rodríguez

Mama gazed out of the back porch window to the garage room where I spent my days holed up as if in a prison of my own making.

She worried about me, although not really knowing what I was up to; to protect herself from being hurt, she stayed uninvolved. Yet almost daily she offered comments about my not attending school.

Mama called on the former principal of my elementary school in South San Gabriel to talk to me. With glasses and bow tie, Mr. Rothro wore unpressed suits which hung on his tall, lean frame. Mama knocked and I invited them in. Mr. Rothro ducked under the doorway and looked around, amazed at the magnificent disorder, the colors and scribble on every wall, the fantastic use of the imagination for such a small room. Mama left and Mr. Rothro, unable to find a place to sit, stood around and provided an encouragement of words. Some very fine words.

"Luis, you've always struck me as an intelligent young man," Mr. Rothro said. "But your mother tells me you're wasting away your days. I'd like to see you back in school. If there's anything constructive I can do—write a letter, make a phone call—perhaps you can return at a level worthy of your gifts."

I sat on a bed in front of an obsolete Royal typewriter with keys that repeatedly got stuck and a carbon ribbon that kept jumping off its latch. My father gave me the typewriter after I found it among boxes, books and personal items in the garage.

"What are you doing?" Mr. Rothro inquired.

"I'm writing a book," I said, matter-of-factly.

"You're what? May I see?"

I let him glimpse at the leaf of paper in the typewriter with barely visible type, full of x's where I crossed out errors as I worked. I didn't know how to type; I just punched the letters I needed with my index fingers. It took me forever to finish a page, but I kept at it in between my other activities. By then I actually had about 125 sheets done.

"What's the book about, son?" Rothro asked.

"Just things. . . what I've seen, what I feel, about the people around me. You know—things."

"Interesting," Rothro said. "In fact, I believe you're probably doing better than most young people—even better, I'm afraid, than some who *are* going to school."

He smiled, said he had to go but if I needed his help, not to hesitate to call.

I acknowledged his goodby and watched him leave the room and walk up to the house, shaking his head. He wasn't the first to wonder about this mystery of a boy, who looked like he could choke the life out of you one minute and then recite a poem in another.

Prior to this, I tried to attend Continuation High School in Alhambra—later renamed Century High to remove the disgrace of being the school for those who couldn't make it anywhere else. After a week, they "let" me go for fighting. When you failed at Continuation, the only place left was the road.

Then my father came up with a plan; when he proposed it, I knew it arose out of desperation.

It consisted of my getting up every day at 4:30 a.m. and going with him to his job at Pierce Junior College in the San Fernando Valley—almost 40 miles away on the other side of Los Angeles. He would enroll me in Taft High School near the college.

I didn't really care so I said sure, why not?

Thus we began our daily trek to a familiar and hostile place—the college was located near Reseda where the family once lived for almost a year. The risk for my father involved me finding out what he really did for a living. Dad told us he worked as a laboratory technician,[1] how a special category had been created at Pierce College for him.

My father worked in the biology labs[2] and maintained the science department's museum and weather station. But to me, he was an overblown janitor. Dad cleaned the cages of snakes, spiders, lizards and other creatures used in the labs. He swept floors and wiped study tables; dusted and mopped the museum area. Dad managed some technical duties such as gathering the weather

[1]Technician: Technical expert.
[2]Labs: Short for laboratories.

station reports, preparing work materials for students, and feeding and providing for the animals. Dad felt proud of his job—but he was only a janitor.

I don't know why this affected me. There's nothing wrong with being a janitor—and one as prestigious as my dad! But for years, I had this running fantasy of my scientist father in a laboratory carrying out vital experiments—the imagination of a worthless kid who wanted so much to break away from the confinements of a society which expected my father to be a janitor or a laborer—when I wanted a father who transformed the world. I had watched too much TV.

One day I walked into the college's science department after school.

"Mr. Rodríguez, you have to be more careful with the placement of laboratory equipment," trembled a professor's stern voice.

"I unnerstan'. . . Sarry. . . I unnerstan'," Dad replied.

"I don't think you do, this is the second time in a month this equipment has not been placed properly."

I glanced over so as not to be seen. My dad looked like a lowly peasant, a man with a hat in his hand—apologetic. At home he was king, *el jefito*—the "word." But here my father turned into somebody else's push-around. Dad should have been equals with anyone, but with such bad English. . .

Oh my father, why don't you stand up to them? Why don't you be the man you are at home?

I turned away and kept on walking.

The opportunity for me to learn something new became an incentive for attending Taft High School. At Keppel and Continuation, I mainly had industrial arts classes. So I applied for classes which stirred a little curiosity: photography, advanced art, and literature. The first day of school, a Taft High School counselor called me into her office.

"I'm sorry, young man, but the classes you chose are filled up," she said.

"What do you mean? Isn't there any way I can get into any of them?"

"I don't believe so. Besides, your records show you're not academically prepared for your choices. These classes are privileges, for those who have maintained the proper grades in the required courses. And I must add, you've obtained most of what credits you do have in industrial-related courses."

"I had to—that's all they'd give me," I said. "I just thought, maybe, I can do something else here. It seems like a good school and I want a chance to do something other than with my hands."

"It doesn't work that way," she expounded. "I think you'll find our industrial arts subjects more suited to your needs."

I shifted in my seat and looked out the window. "Whatever."

The classes she enrolled me in were print shop, auto shop and weight training. I did manage a basic English literature class. I walked past the photography sessions and stopped to glimpse the students going in and out, some with nice cameras, and I thought about how I couldn't afford those cameras anyway: *Who needs that stupid class?*

In print shop I worked the area where lead was melted for the mechanical Linotype typesetter. I received scars on my arms due to splashes of molten lead. In auto shop I did a lot of tune-ups, oil changes and some transmission work. And I lifted weights and started to bulk up. The one value I had was being the only Mexican in school—people talked about it whenever I approached.

One day at lunch time, I passed a number of big guys in lettered jackets. One of them said something. Maybe it had nothing to do with me. But I pounced on him anyway. Several teachers had to pull me off.

They called me violent and out of control; they didn't know "what to do with me."

After school, I walked to Pierce College and waited for Dad to finish his work so we could go home, which usually went past dark. I spent many evenings in the library. But I found most books boring.

I picked up research and history books and went directly to the index and looked up "Mexican." If there were a few items under this topic, I read them; I read them all.

Every day I browsed, ventured into various sections of shelves; most of this struck me with little interest. One evening, I came across a crop of new books on a special shelf near the front of the library. I picked one up, then two. The librarian looked at me through the side of her eye, as if she kept tabs on whoever examined those books.

They were primarily about the black experience, works coming out of the flames which swallowed up many American cities in the 1960s. I discovered Claude Brown's *Manchild in the Promised Land*, Eldridge Cleaver's *Soul on Ice*, and the *Autobiography of Malcom X*. I found poetry by Don L. Lee and LeRoi Jones (now known as Haki R. Madhubuti and Amiri Baraka). And a few books by Puerto Ricans and Chicanos: Victor Hernández Cruz's *Snaps* and Ricardo Sánchez's *Canto Y Grito: Mi Liberacion*[3] were two of them. Here were books with a connection to me.

And then there was Piri Thomas, a Puerto Rican brother: His book *Down These Mean Streets* became a living Bible for me. I dog-eared it, wrote in it, copied whole passages so I wouldn't forget their structure, the passion, this scorching work of a street boy in Spanish Harlem—a barrio[4] boy like me, on the other side of America.

One day I came in slightly late to my English literature class and sat down; I placed a book on top of the desk. The teacher walked up to me and picked up the book.

"*American Me* by Beatrice Griffith," he said. "Where did you get this book?"

"It's a library book—it's about the *pachuco*[5] experience in the 1940s."

"Sounds good, but the book you were to bring here today was Wordsworth's *Preludes*. That is your assignment, not *American Me*."

[3]*Canto Y Grito: Mi Liberacion:* I Sing and Scream: My Liberation.

[4]Barrio: Section of a city inhabited chiefly by Spanish-speaking people.

[5]*Pachuco*: Member of a Mexican-American neighborhood gang.

"This book is something I'd like to read. I can even do a report on it."

"Young man, you don't decide your assignments in this class. If you can't participate like the rest of us, I suggest you leave."

"Fine—who cares what I want!"

I stormed out of there. Needless to say, this was my last day in the class.

But the teachers' strike of 1970 was the real reason I stopped going to Taft. The strike lasted a couple of months. But when the teachers settled with the Los Angeles School Board, I stayed out; I felt the school district hadn't settled with me yet.

I ended up back in the streets. Somehow, though, it wasn't the same as before. A power pulsed in those books I learned to appreciate, in the magical hours I spent in the library—and it called me back to them.

Sometimes I roamed the street with nothing to do and ended up in a library. Later on my own I picked up Wordsworth, Poe, Emerson and Whitman.

I also learned not to be angry with my father. I learned something about my father's love, which he never expressed in words, but instead, at great risk, he gave me the world of books—a gift for a lifetime.

The Jewels of

by Guy de Maupassant

M. Lantin, having met this young lady at a party given by his immediate superior, directly fell in love.

She was the daughter of a tax collector who had died a few years previously. With her mother, she had come to Paris. Her mother became friendly with several middle-class families of the neighborhood in hopes of marrying off the young lady. Mother and daughter were poor, honorable, quiet, and gentle. The girl seemed to be the typical dream woman with whom any young man would yearn to spend his entire life. Her modest beauty was like an angel's, and the smile that constantly graced her lips seemed a reflection of her heart.

Everyone sang her praises; everyone who knew her repeated constantly: "It will be a lucky fellow who wins her. You couldn't find a better catch!"

M. Lantin, now chief clerk of the Minister of the Interior, at a salary of 3500 francs,[1] asked and received her hand in marriage.

He was unbelievably happy. She managed the house with such skill that their life was one of luxury. There was no whim of her husband's that she did not secure and satisfy; and her personal charm was such that, six years after their first meeting, he loved her more than he had initially.

[1]Francs: French money.

M. Lantin

He begrudged her only two traits—her love of the theater and her passion for artificial jewels.

Her friends (she knew the wives of several minor officials) were always getting her seats for fashionable plays, sometimes even for first nights; and she dragged her poor husband to these entertainments, which completely wore him out, tired as he was after a hard day's work. He begged her to agree to go to the theater with some lady friend of hers who would accompany her home. She took a long time to decide, claiming this a most inconvenient arrangement. At last, however, she agreed, and he was profoundly grateful to her.

Now, this taste for the theater naturally stirred in her the need to dress up. Her attire remained simple, to be sure—always modest but in good taste; but she became accustomed to wearing two huge rhinestone earrings, which looked like diamonds. She had strings of artificial pearls around her neck and wore bracelets of similar gems.

Her husband, who somewhat scorned this love of display, said, "Dearest, when you haven't the means to wear real jewelry, you should show yourself adorned only with your own grace and beauty; these are the true pearls."

But she, smiling quietly, would insist, "Can I help it? I love it so. This is my vice. I know, my dear, how absolutely right you are; but I can't really remake myself, can I?"

And she would roll the pearls in her fingers. "See how perfect," she'd say. "You'd swear they were real."

Sometimes, during the evening, while they sat before the fire, she would bring out her jewel chest and examine the contents with passionate attention, as though there were some subtle and profound secret delight in this pursuit. She persisted in draping strings of pearls around her

husband's neck; then she would laugh merrily, crying, "How silly you look, my darling!" And she would throw herself into his arms and kiss him wildly.

One wintry evening, when she had been at the opera, she came home shivering with cold. The next day she was coughing wretchedly. A week later she died.

Lantin nearly followed her into the tomb. His despair was such that, in a month's time, his hair turned completely white. He wept continuously, haunted by the memory, the smile, the voice, the beauty of his dead wife.

Even the passage of time failed to stem his grief. He kept his wife's room unchanged. All her furniture and even her dresses remained just where they had been on the fatal day.

Living became difficult for him. His income which, under his wife's management, supplied the needs of both, now became too little for him alone. Dazed, he wondered how she had been able to purchase the superb wines he could no longer afford.

He fell into debt and began to scurry around for money as does anyone suddenly plunged into poverty. One morning, finding himself penniless a full week before payday, he thought about selling something. Suddenly the idea swept over him of taking a look at his wife's treasure chest, because, if the truth be told, he had always harbored some resentment towards this store of brilliants. The mere sight of them slightly tarnished the memory of his beloved.

It was a difficult business, searching through the case of jewels. He finally chose the magnificent necklace she seemed to have preferred, which, he figured, was worth six or seven francs, because, for artificial gems, it was really a masterpiece.

With the jewels in his pocket, he looked for a reliable jeweler.

Spotting a store, he entered—somewhat sad to be making this public display of his poverty and ashamed at attempting to sell so worthless an object.

The man took the necklace, turned it over, weighed it, called to his partner, talked to him in low tones, placed the necklace on the counter, and examined it carefully from a distance as though judging the effect.

M. Lantin, embarrassed by this process, opened his mouth to protest: "I know that piece isn't worth anything," but just at that moment the storekeeper said: "This piece is worth between twelve and fifteen thousand francs, but I cannot buy it until I learn exactly how you came into possession of it."

Lantin stared, wide-eyed. He finally stammered, "What? You are absolutely sure?"

The gentleman seemed offended by his attitude. "You may go elsewhere if you think you can do better. To me that is worth fifteen thousand at the very most. If you find no better offer, you may come back here."

M. Lantin took the necklace and left, feeling a curious urge to be alone and undisturbed.

But before he had gone far, he was seized with an impulse to laugh, and he thought, "Fool! What if I had taken him at his word! What a jeweler—not to know the difference between real gems and fakes!"

And he entered another store. As soon as he saw the jewel, the dealer cried, "Of course! I know this necklace well; I sold it!"

Deeply disturbed, M. Lantin asked, "How much is it worth?"

"Sir, I sold it for twenty-five thousand francs. I'm ready to take it back for eighteen thousand, if you will tell me—the law, you know—how you happened to receive it."

This time Lantin sat paralyzed with astonishment. He stuttered, "But—examine it very closely. I have always thought it was—artificial."

The jeweler asked, "Would you please tell me your name, sir."

"Of course, I'm Lantin. I work at the Ministry of the Interior, and I live at 16 Rue des Martyrs."

The merchant opened his ledger, looked through it, and said, "This necklace was sent to Mme. Lantin, 16 Rue des Martyrs, on the twentieth of July, 1876."

The two men stared at each other.

The merchant said, "Would you mind letting me have this for a day? Naturally, I'll give you a receipt."

M. Lantin burst out, "Of course!" and left.

His wife could not possibly have purchased such valuable jewelry. Absolutely not! Well then? A present? From whom? For what?

He was brought up short—there in the middle of the street. A horrible thought flashed across his mind. She? But all those other jewels were also gifts! He felt the earth shiver; a tree just before him seemed to crush him. He threw out his arms and fell, senseless, to the ground.

He regained consciousness in a nearby pharmacy to which passersby had carried him. He asked that he be taken home, and he locked himself in.

He wept bitterly until nightfall—stuffing a handkerchief into his mouth to stifle his cries. Then he staggered to bed, wrung out with fatigue and sorrow, and he slept heavily.

A ray of sunshine woke him, and he got up slowly to go to his office. After such a blow, it would be hard to carry on with his work. He wrote his superior a note. Then he thought that he ought to go back to the jeweler; and he crimsoned with shame. He could not possibly leave the necklace with that man. He dressed hurriedly and went out.

As he walked along, Lantin said to himself, "How easy it is to be happy when you're rich! With money you can even shake off your sorrows. You can travel and amuse yourself. If only I were really rich!"

Then he became aware of the fact that he was hungry, not having eaten since the previous evening. But his pockets were empty, and he reminded himself of the necklace. Eighteen thousand francs! What a fortune!

He reached the shop and began pacing up and down opposite it. Eighteen thousand francs! More than twenty times he started to enter; but shame always halted him.

He was still hungry—and without a penny. He finally made up his mind, raced across the street so as not to give himself time to think, and burst into the store.

As soon as he saw him, the merchant greeted him royally, offered him a chair with smiling courtesy. The partners then came in and sat down near Lantin, happiness beaming from their eyes and their lips.

The jeweler declared, "I am satisfied, Monsieur, and if you feel as you did yesterday, I am ready to pay you the sum agreed upon."

"Certainly," stammered Lantin.

The merchant took eighteen large notes from a drawer, counted them, gave them to Lantin, who signed a receipt and, with trembling hand, stuffed the money into his pocket.

Then, just as he was going out, he turned back towards the shopkeeper and, lowering his eyes, murmured, "I—I have some other gems—which came to me in the same way. Would you be willing to buy those from me?"

The jeweler nodded. "Of course, Monsieur."

When he returned to the store, an hour later, he had still not eaten. They set about examining the jewels piece by piece, pricing each one. Then they all went back to Lantin's house.

Now Lantin entered into the spirit of the business, arguing, insisting that they show him the bills of sale, and getting more and more excited as the values rose.

The magnificent earrings were worth twenty thousand francs; the bracelets, thirty-five thousand. The whole collection was valued at one hundred ninety-six thousand francs.

The merchant boomed out in a jolly voice, "That's what happens when you put your money into jewelry."

M. Lantin went into an elegant restaurant to eat, and he drank wine at twenty francs a bottle. Then he took a cab and rode around. He looked at the gleaming carriages, controlling a desire to cry out, "I'm rich, too! I have two hundred thousand francs!"

He thought of his office. He drove up, entered his chief's office solemnly, and announced, "Sir, I'm handing in my resignation! I've just inherited three hundred thousand francs!" He went around shaking hands with his co-workers and telling them all about his plans for the future. Then he went out to dinner at an expensive café.

Finding himself seated alongside a distinguished-looking gentleman, he couldn't resist whispering to him that he had just inherited four hundred thousand francs.

For the first time in his life he enjoyed the theater, and he spent the night partying.

Six months later he remarried. His second wife was a most worthy woman, but rather difficult. She made his life unbearable.

A Start in Life

Part 1
by Ruth Suckow

The Switzers were scurrying around to get Daisy ready by the time that Elmer Kruse should get in town. They had known all week that Elmer might be in for her any day. But they hadn't done a thing until he appeared. "Oh, it was so rainy today, the roads were so muddy, they hadn't thought he'd get it until maybe next week." It would have been the same any other day.

Mrs. Switzer was trying now at the last moment to get all of Daisy's things into the battered bag that lay on the bed. The bed had not "got made"; and just as soon as Daisy was gone, Mrs. Switzer would have to hurry off to the Woodworths, where she was to wash today. Daisy's things were scattered over the wrinkled sheets that were dingy and clammy in this damp weather. So was the whole bedroom with its sloping ceiling, the dresser littered with curlers, broken combs, ribbons, smoky lamp, all mixed up together; the door of the closet open, showing the confusion of clothes and shabby shoes. They all slept in this room—Mrs. Switzer and Dwight in the bed, the two girls in the cot against the wall.

"Mama, I can't find the belt to that plaid dress."

"Oh, ain't it somewheres around? Well, I guess you'll have to let it go. If I come across it, I can send it out to you. Someone'll be going past there."

She had meant to get Daisy all mended and "fixed up" before she went out to the country. But somehow—oh, there was always so much to see to when she came home. Gone all day, washing and cleaning for other people; it didn't leave her much time for her own home.

She was late now. The Woodworths liked to have her get the washing out early so that she could do some cleaning, too, before she left. But she couldn't help it. She would have to get Daisy off first. She had already had on her wraps ready to go, when Elmer came—her cleaning cap, of a blue faded almost gray, and the ancient black coat that she wore over her work dress when she went out to wash.

"What's become of all your underclothes? They ain't all dirty, are they?"

"They are too. You didn't wash for us last week, Mama."

"Well, you'll just have to take along what you've got. Maybe there'll be some way of getting the rest to you."

"Elmer comes in every week, doesn't he?" Daisy demanded.

"Yes, but maybe he won't always be bringing you in." She jammed what she could into the bag, thinking that it would have to do somehow. "You needn't be so anxious to fix yourself up. This ain't like going visiting."

Daisy stood at the little mirror—such a homely child, "all Switzer," skinny, with pale sharp eyes set close together and thin, stringy, reddish hair. But she had never really learned yet how homely she was. She was the oldest, and she got the pick of what clothes were given to the Switzers. Goldie and Dwight envied her. She was important in her small world. She was proud of her blue coat that had belonged to Alice Brooker, the town lawyer's daughter. It hung unevenly above her bony little knees, and the buttons came down too far. Her mother had tried to make it over for her.

Mrs. Switzer looked at her, troubled, but not knowing how she could tell her all the things she ought to be told. Daisy had never been away before except to go to her Uncle Fred's at Lehigh. She seemed to think that this would be the same. She had so many things to learn. Well, she would find them out soon enough—only too soon. Working for other people—she would learn what that meant. Elmer and Edna Kruse were nice young people. They would mean well enough by Daisy. It was a good chance for her to start in. But it wasn't the same.

Daisy was so proud. She thought it was quite a thing to be "starting in to earn." She thought she could buy herself so much with her dollar and a half a week. The other children stood back watching her, round-eyed and impressed. They wished that they were going away, like Daisy.

They heard a car come splashing through the mud. "There he is! Have you got your things on? Goldie, go out and tell him she's coming."

"No, me tell him, me!" Dwight shouted jealously.

"Well, both of you tell him. Land!"

She tried hastily to put on the cover of the bulging bag and to fasten the straps. One of them broke.

"Well, I guess you'll have to go now. He won't want to wait. I'll try and send out what you ain't got with you." She turned to Daisy. Her face was working. There was nothing else to do, as everyone said. Daisy would have to help, and she might as well learn it now. Only, she hated to see Daisy go off, to have her starting in. She knew what it meant. "Well, you try and work good this summer, so they'll want you to stay. I hope they'll bring you in sometimes."

Daisy's homely little face grew pale with awe, suddenly, at the sight of her mother crying.

Elmer's big new Buick, mud-splashed but imposing, stood on the uneven road. Mud was thick on the wheels. It was a bad day for driving. The little road that led past these few houses on the outskirts of town had a cold, rainy loneliness. Elmer sat in the front seat of the Buick, and in the back was a big box of groceries.

"Got any room to sit in there?" he asked genially. "I didn't get out, it's so muddy here."

"No, don't get out," Mrs. Switzer said hastily. "She can put this right on the floor there in the back." She added, with a timid attempt at courtesy, "Ain't the roads pretty bad out that way?"

"Yes, but farmers get so they don't think so much about the roads."

"I s'pose that's so."

He saw the signs of tears on Mrs. Switzer's face, and they made him anxious to get away. She embraced Daisy hastily again. Daisy climbed over the grocery box and squeezed herself into the seat.

"I guess you'll bring her in with you sometime when you're coming," Mrs. Switzer hinted.

"Sure. We'll bring her."

He started the engine.

In that moment, Daisy had a startled view of home—the small house standing on a rough rise of land, weathered to a dim color that showed dark streaks from the rain; the narrow, sloping front porch, whose edge had a soaked, gnawed look; the chickens, grayish-black, pecking at the wet ground; their playthings, stones, a wagon, some old pail covers littered about; a soaked, discolored piece of underwear hanging on the line in the backyard. Goldie and Dwight were gazing at her solemnly. She saw her mother's face—a thin, weak, loving face, drawn with neglected weeping, with its reddened eyes and poor teeth; the old coat and heavy shoes and cleaning cap; her work-worn hand with its big knuckles clutching at her coat. She saw the playthings they had used yesterday, and the old swing that hung from one of the trees.

The car went off, slipping on the wet clay. Daisy waved frantically, suddenly understanding that she was leaving them. They waved at her.

Mrs. Switzer stood there a little while. Then came the harsh sound of the old black iron pump that stood out under the tree. She was pumping water to leave for the children before she went off to work.

Daisy held on as the car skidded down the short clay hill. Her eyes brightened with scared excitement. She looked back, holding on her hat with her small thin hand.

Just down this little hill—and home was gone. The big car, the feel of her bag on the floor under her feet, the fact that she was going out to the country, changed the looks of everything. She saw it all now.

Dunkels' house stood on one side of the road—a closed-up white house. The windows stared blank and cold between the old shutters. There was a chair with a broken straw seat under the fruit trees. In the front yard was a clump of tall pines, the ground underneath mournfully wet and black.

They slid onto the main road. They bumped over the small wooden bridge above the swollen creek that came from the pasture. Daisy looked down. She saw the little swirls of foam, the long grass that swished with the water, the old rusted tin cans lodged between the rocks.

She sat up straight and important, her thin, homely little face strained with excitement, her sharp eyes taking in everything.

She felt the magnificence of having a ride. One wet Sunday Mr. Brooker had driven them all home from church, she and Goldie and Dwight. Sometimes they could plan to go to town just when Mr. Pattey was going to work in his Ford. Then they would run out and shout eagerly, "Mr. Pattey! Are you going through town?" Sometimes he said good-naturedly, "Well, pile in," and they all hopped into the truck back.

She looked at the black wet fields through which little leaves of bright green corn grew in rows. A gasoline engine pumping water made a loud desolate sound. There were sad-looking cattle in the wet grass, and lonely trees growing here and there in the pastures. She felt her bag on the floor of the car, the box of groceries beside her. She eyed these with a sharp curiosity. There was a fresh pineapple—something the Switzers didn't often get at home. She wondered if Edna would have it for dinner. Maybe she could hint a little to Edna.

She was out in the country. She could no longer see her house even if she wanted to—standing dingy, streaked with rain, in its rough grass on the little hill. A lump came into her throat. She had looked forward to playing with Edna's children. But Goldie and Dwight would play all morning without her. She was still proud of going out with Elmer and Edna, but now there was a forlornness in the pride.

She wished she were in the front seat with Elmer. She didn't see why he hadn't put her there. Elmer must have lots of money to buy a car like this. He had a new house on his farm, too, and Mrs. Metzinger had said that it had plumbing. Maybe they would take her to the movies. She might hint about that.

She looked at Elmer's back, the old felt hat carelessly on his head, his hands on the steering wheel that he handled so masterly. Elmer and Edna were just young folks; but Mrs. Metzinger said that they had more to start with than most young farmers did, and that they were hustlers. Daisy felt that the pride of this belonged to her too, now.

"Here we are!"

"Oh, is this where you folks live?" Daisy cried eagerly.

The house stood back from the road, beyond a space of bare yard with a little scattering of grass just starting—small, modern, painted a bright new white and yellow. The barn was new too, a big splendid barn of brick. There were no trees. A raw, desolate wind blew across the backyard as they drove up beside the back door.

End of Part 1

A Start in Life

Part 2
by Ruth Suckow

Edna came out on the step. Elmer grinned at her as he took out the box of groceries, and she slightly raised her eyebrows. She said kindly enough: "Well, you brought Daisy. Hello, Daisy. So you're going to stay with us this summer?"

"I guess so," Daisy said importantly. But she suddenly felt a little shy as she got out of the car and stood on the bare ground in the chilly wind.

Two little round heads were pressed tightly against the screen door. There was a clamor of "Daddy, Daddy!" Elmer grinned with bashful pride as he stood with the box of groceries, raising his eyebrows with mock surprise and demanding, "You don't think Daddy's got anything for you, do you?" He and Edna were going into the kitchen together, until Edna remembered and called back hastily: "Oh, come in, Daisy."

Daisy stood, a little left out and solitary, there in the kitchen, as Billy, the older of the babies, climbed frantically over Elmer, demanding candy, and the little one waddled smilingly about. Her eyes took in all of it. She was impressed by the shining linoleum, the stove with its nickel and enamel, the bright new woodwork. Edna was laughing and scolding at Elmer and the baby. Billy had made his father produce the candy. Daisy's sharp little eyes looked hungrily at the lemon drops, and Edna remembered her: "Give Daisy a piece of your candy," she said.

He would not go up to Daisy. She had to come forward and take one of the lemon drops herself. She saw where Edna put the sack, in a dish high in the cupboard. She hoped they would get some more before long.

"My bag's out there in the car," she reminded them.

"Oh! Elmer, you go and get it and take it up for her," Edna said.

"What?"

"Her valise—or whatever it is—out in the car."

"It's kind of an old bag," Daisy said conversationally. "I guess it's been used a lot. The strap broke when Mama was fastening it this morning. We ain't got any suitcase. I had to take this because it was all there was in the house, and Mama didn't want to get me a new one."

Edna raised her eyebrows politely. She leaned over and patted the baby.

Daisy watched solemnly. "I didn't know both of your children was boys."

"Um-hm," Edna replied absently. "You can unpack your valise now, I guess, if you'd like to. Then you can come down and help me in the kitchen. You know we got you to help me," she reminded.

Daisy, subdued, followed Elmer up the bright new stairs.

She looked about her room with intense curiosity. It had a bright varnished floor. She had a bed all her own—a small, old-fashioned bed that had been put in this room that had the pipes and the hot water tank. She had to see everything, but she was uncomfortable as she tiptoed about and started to open the drawers of the dresser. She put her coat and hat on the bed. She would rather be down in the kitchen with Edna than unpack her bag now.

She guessed she would go down where the rest of them were.

Later in the day, Elmer came into the house for dinner. He brought in a cold, muddy, outdoor breath with him. The stove was going, but the bright little kitchen seemed chilly.

Edna made a significant little face at Elmer. Daisy did not see. She was standing back from the stove, where Edna was at work, looking at the baby.

"He can talk pretty good, can't he? Dwight couldn't say anything but 'Mama' when he was that little."

Edna's back was turned. She said meaningly: "Now, Elmer's come in for dinner, Daisy, we'll have to hurry. You can cut bread and get things on the table. You must help, you know. That's what you are supposed to do."

Daisy looked startled, a little scared, and resentful. "Well, I don't know where you keep your bread."

"Don't you remember where I told you to put it this morning? Right over in the cabinet. You must watch, Daisy, and learn where things are."

Elmer, a little embarrassed at the look that Edna gave him, whistled as he began to wash his hands at the sink.

As Enda passed him, she shook her head and her lips just formed, "Been like that all morning!"

He grinned understandingly.

Daisy had not exactly heard, but she looked from one to the other, silent and wondering. The queer ache that had kept starting all through the morning came over her again.

"I guess I'm going to have the toothache again," she said faintly.

No one seemed to hear her.

Edna whisked off the potatoes. "You might bring me a dish, Daisy." Daisy searched a long time while Edna turned impatiently and pointed. Edna put the rest of the things on the table herself. Her young, fresh, capable mouth was tightly closed, and she was making certain resolutions.

Daisy stood hesitating in the middle of the room, an unappealing little figure. Billy was trotting busily about the kitchen. Daisy swooped down upon him and tired to bring him to the table. He set up a howl. Edna turned, looked astonished, severe.

"I was trying to make him come to the table," Daisy explained weakly.

"You scared him. He isn't used to you. Don't cry, Billy. The girl didn't mean anything."

Daisy felt strangely at a loss. She had been left with Goldie and Dwight so often. She had always made Dwight go to the table.

Edna said in a cool voice, "Put these things on the table, Daisy."

They sat down. Daisy and the other children had always felt it a great treat to eat away from home. They had hung around Mrs. Metzinger's house at noon, hoping to be asked to stay, not offended when told that "it was time for them to run off now." Her pinched little face had a hungry look as she stared at the potatoes and ham and pie. But they did not watch and urge her to have more, as Mrs. Metzinger did, and Mrs. Brooker when she took pity on the Switzers and had them there. Daisy wanted more pie. But none of them seemed to be taking more, and so she said nothing. She remembered what her mother had said, now with a faint understanding. "You're working for other folks, and it won't be like it is at home."

After dinner Edna said, "Now you can wash the dishes, Daisy."

Daisy, as she went hesitatingly about the kitchen alone, could hear Edna's contented humming. The bright kitchen was empty and lonely.

She finished as soon as she could and went into the dining room. Edna was sewing. That queer low ache went all through her. She said in a small dismal voice: "I guess I got the toothache again."

Edna bit off a thread.

"I had it awful hard awhile ago. Mama came pretty near taking me to the dentist."

"That's too bad," Edna murmured politely. But she offered no other sympathy. She gave a little secret smile at the baby asleep on a blanket in a corner of the leather couch.

"Is Elmer going to drive into town tomorrow?"

"Tomorrow? I don't suppose so."

"Mama couldn't find the belt of my plaid dress, and I thought if he was, maybe I could go along and get it."

Daisy's homely little mouth drooped at the corners. Her toothache did not seem to matter to anyone. Edna did not seem to want to see that anything was wrong with her.

She saw Mama's face as in that last glimpse of it—drawn with crying, and yet trying to smile.

Edna glanced at her. The child was so unattractive, unappealing even in her forlornness. Edna frowned a little, but said kindly: "Now you might take Billy into the kitchen out of my way, Daisy, and amuse him."

"Well, he cries when I pick him up," Daisy said faintly.

"He won't cry this time. Take him and help him play with his blocks."

Billy nodded. Daisy felt a thrill of comfort as Billy put his hand in hers and trottted beside her.

She set out the blocks on the bright linoleum. She had never had such blocks as these to handle before. Her spirit of leadership came back, and she firmly put Billy's hand away whenever he meddled with her building. She knew what she was going to make—it was going to be a house; no, a church. Just as she got the walls up, Billy swept the blocks to the floor.

Daisy picked him up and firmly transplanted him to another corner of the room. He set up a tremendous howl. Edna came hurrying out.

"Billy knocked over the blocks. He spoiled the building. I didn't hurt him," Daisy said, scared.

"They're Billy's blocks, Daisy. He doesn't like to sit and see you put up buildings."

"I didn't hurt him," Daisy protested.

"Well, never mind now. You can pick up the blocks and then sweep the floor. You didn't do that when you finished the dishes. Never mind," she was saying to Billy. "Pretty soon Daddy'll come in, and we'll have a nice ride."

Daisy picked up the blocks. What had she done to Billy? She had always made Dwight keep back until she had finished building. She winked back tears.

Then she brightened as Elmer came tramping up on the back porch.

"Edna! Want to go now?"

Edna gave him a warning look, and the door was closed.

Daisy listened hard. She swept very softly. She could catch only a little of what they said—"Kind of hate to go off . . . But if we once start . . . not a thing all day . . . what we got her for . . ." She had no real understanding of it. She hurried and put away the broom. She wanted to be sure and be ready to go.

Elmer tramped out, straight past her. She saw from the window that he was backing the car out from the shed.

Elmer honked the horn. A moment later Edna came hurrying downstairs. She did not look at Daisy, but said hurriedly, "We're going for a little ride, Daisy. Have you finished sweeping? Well, then, you can pick up in the dining room. We won't be gone very long. When it's a quarter past five, start the fire like I showed you this noon, and slice the potatoes and the meat. And set the table."

The horn was honked again.

Daisy stood looking after them. Billy clamored to sit beside his daddy. Edna put the baby beside her on the back seat. There was room—half of the big back seat. There wasn't anything, really, to be done at home. That was the worst of it. They just didn't want to take her.

She went forlornly into the dining room. The light from the windows was dim now in the rainy, late afternoon.

The dreadful ache submerged her. No one would ask about it, no one would try to comfort her. Before, there had always been Mama coming home, anxious, scolding sometimes, but worried over them if they didn't feel right. Mama and Goldie and Dwight cared about her—but Daisy was away out in the country, and they were at home. She didn't want to stay here, where she didn't belong. But Mama had told her that she must begin helping this summer.

Her ugly little mouth twisted with weeping. But silent weeping, without any tears; because she already had the cold knowledge that no one would notice or comfort it.

Skyjacked

by Mike McGrady

American Airlines Flight 626 was an hour out of New York. It was this past New Year's Eve—normally a day off for pilot Ken Korshin, but the company had talked him into filling in on the St. Croix-to-New York flight.

The passengers' festive mood was contagious, and the crew was in high spirits, heading back to New York and waiting celebrations.

When the cockpit door opened, Korshin knew it would be flight attendant Bonnie Dotter with the hot coffee. It was Bonnie, all right, but there was no coffee. Bonnie's face seemed pale and her voice was overly steady, consciously steady.

"There's a man holding a gun to a man on the floor."

No time to react properly. A man holding a gun to a man on the floor? Who was holding a gun on whom? The pilot knew there was a prisoner aboard—was he the one holding the gun or was one of the guards holding a gun on him?

Two rings on the interphone. It was the voice of the No. 1 flight attendant, Jean Keiser. In spite of her effort to control her emotion, the tremble came through. The sentences came in abrupt bursts: "Ken, this is Jean. The prisoner has a gun to my head. He wants you to come back here. He says we're going to Havana, Ken. This is no joke. He is for real."

Just that quickly Korshin's mouth went dry and an icicle of fear stabbed through him.

"Let me speak to him," Korshin said. Going back and joining him in the rear of the aircraft—that was an option to be avoided. If possible.

"I'm Ishmael Ali—you know who I am?" He didn't have to elaborate, but he did. "I'm the Fountain Valley Murderer."

Ishmael Ali. His name in the newspapers had been Ishmael Ali LaBeet. Anyone who flew regularly into the islands knew the story of the Fountain Valley murders. That 1972 incident altered the social scenery of St. Croix and the Virgin Islands. Ishmael Ali LaBeet, 37, was a black revolutionary. One September morning, in order to demonstrate against the oppression of blacks in the Virgin Islands, he had, with four friends, gone out onto St. Croix's Foundatin Valley Golf Course with a machine gun and butchered eight people.

"I know who you are."

"Fine, now if you don't turn this plane around, I'm going to shoot somebody."

Korshin turned to Scott Chamier, a fellow supervisory captain sharing the flight, and mouthed the word: "Hijack." Then, a second later, "Turn . . . now!" The two pilots never questioned whether LaBeet would carry out his threat. This was a convicted mass murderer sentenced to eight consecutive life sentences, a man with nothing to lose. The aircraft began its broad U-turn. Chamier got on the radio and told the world that American Airlines Flight 626, St. Croix to New York, was being skyjacked.

LaBeet had ordered the three disarmed guards to sit together directly in front of him at the rear of the plane. Flight attendant Jean Keiser took over the public address system and repeated LaBeet's instructions to the passengers: They were to buckle their seat belts, look straight ahead, refrain from talking, and keep their hands crossed on top of the seats in front of them. If they wanted to get out of their seats for any reason, they had to raise their hands and ask permission. If they wanted to use the lavatory, the door must be kept open. No one would be hurt if instructions were followed.

"Mr. Ali," Korshin said, "we're a little short of fuel, and I really don't feel we have enough to make Havana."

"Don't give me that low-on-fuel story," he said. "We're not landing anywhere except Havana. Or the sea."

LeBeet's notion that the pilot was lying about the fuel was not at all far-fetched. Korshin's instinct would have been to claim a fuel shortage no matter what the true situation. In this case, however, he couldn't be sure. He was waiting for the third man in the cockpit, Flight Engineer Hal Tiedemann, to get a handle on the fuel situation.

"It looks like we're going to have about nine or ten thousand over the station," Tiedemann said. They would, then, land in Havana with 10,000 pounds of fuel, enough for an additional 50 minutes of flight.

By this time, communications had been established in New York.

"This is American 626. Hijacking in progress. It's real, it's serious, the man is armed and dangerous, and we are proceeding to Havana. We are climbing to 36,000 feet. Our last position was 33 degrees 5 minutes north and 72 degrees and 24 minutes west. Would you please get the company." Later, they provided the identity of their hijacker—Ishmael Ali LaBeet, the Fountain Valley Murderer.

The message from Flight 626 set many wheels in motion. The minute a hijacking is reported, a command center is set up by the airline—in this case at Dallas-Fort Worth, corporate headquarters for American Airlines.

The command center talks with the pilots, the FBI, the State Department, air controllers, the FAA, and any other involved parties.

The dryness in Korshin's mouth was intense. He thought briefly of the New Year's Eve dinner waiting for him at home. Prime steak.

As the plane settled into the normal routines of flight, Korshin called LaBeet on the interphone.

"Mr. Ali, we're on the way to Havana," he said. "Although it's close, there's going to be enough fuel."

"Okay," LaBeet said. "I want to hear the Havana tower." After that, LaBeet refused to answer the interphone. And, in fact, he seemed somewhat angered by the pilots' frequent calls to the flight attendants.

"What's all that ringing about?" he asked one of the flight attendants.

"Oh, you know how pilots are. They always want a cup of coffee."

"Well, look, if he's bothering you, I'll just go up there and kill him."

"Oh, no, no, no," she said. "No need to do that. He's a real nice guy."

Korshin and Chamier didn't realize how much the passengers knew about the situation. It was time to give them the specifics—and also time to advise the hijacker that they would be approaching Havana. As Korshin picked up the microphone, he had to steel himself. This was the first time he had ever had to make an announcement when he no longer had control over what was going on in the airplane.

"Ladies and gentlemen, this is the captain," he began. "We have a gentleman on board who has asked to go to Havana, and we are in the process of taking him there. Mr. Ali, if you like, you can listen to the controllers on the cabin headsets. The lights of Miami are off to the right, and we should be landing in Havana in about 25 minutes."

The interphone rang once, twice, three times, four times. Four bells is the signal for an emergency, and none of the men had ever heard it before. "Four bells!" Chamier exclaimed. What had happened? Had someone done something foolish? Three times Ken Korshin's heart stopped during this experience. The first was when he realized a man with a gun had taken control of the airplane. This was the second time. He picked up the receiver and heard a flight attendant's voice: "They're coming up."

The next instant, the cockpit door exploded open and Jean Keiser was saying, "We're here!"

Korshin's first impression? It was snub-nosed, shining, black, a gun barrel pointed directly at Korshin's head.

The man? He got no more than a quick glance, but LaBeet seemed tall, over 6 feet 2 inches, lean and mean, obviously in good shape. He was behind Korshin, off to the left side, and he wore a sport shirt, had a beard. But all Korshin could think was: "This is no way to have to land an airplane."

"How are you doing, Mr. Ali," Korshin said. "Over there's Havana."

"Okay," he said. The flight engineer had started to retrieve a chart from his bag and LaBeet's voice barked out in the cockpit. "Keep your hands where I can see them or I'll blow you away." His tone was different now, and Korshin had a revelation: He was as scared as they were.

"American 626, would you like a straight-in to Runway 23?"

"Affirmative, we'll accept that."

"Roger, call us when you have us in sight."

A moment later: "Havana, this is American 626, we don't have the airport in sight."

"Roger, continue."

Again, an increase in tension in the cockpit. Korshin could sense LaBeet's right hand tightening the back of his seat. The hijacker didn't say a word, but the tension was as real as if he had said, "What do you mean, you don't *see* the airport?"

"Havana, this is American 626," Chamier said. "Would you turn the lights up?"

They blinked on, two strips of white lights about 10 miles straight ahead, yellow through the haze. These were the runway edge lights. There were no approach lights. All Korshin could think was: Three to four minutes and it's all going to be over. Just three or four more minutes. Get the airplane on the ground and it will be over—maybe. Korshin turned to LaBeet. "Mr. Ali, would you mind sitting down and fastening your seat belt?" No reply. "I don't want you to fall," Korshin said in his pilot's voice. "I don't want the gun going off and someone getting hurt." Still no response. "If you don't sit down and fasten your seat belt, please brace yourself against the seat because I don't want you to fall." LeBeet didn't say a word, but again the pilot could feel his hand behind the seat as he braced himself.

By this time, they could see activity at the airport. A group of vehicles was gathering at the end of the runway.

The landing itself was smooth, but to the crew, it seemed to be happening in slow motion. The final half-mile seemed to take an hour instead of just a few seconds. They parked the airplane on a rough ramp lined with fire engines and military vehicles.

LaBeet told them to tell the tower who he was: "Say that I am a political prisoner from the U.S. Virgin Islands seeking asylum in the People's Republic of Cuba." Chamier made the call, as instructed, but the tower operator seemed not to understand. LaBeet asked for a microphone, and this time, he made the statement in slow, carefully pronounced Spanish, and this time, he was understood

"Mr. Ali," Korshin asked, "can I shut the engines down now?"

"Okay."

Korshin turned to LaBeet: "What do you want us to do now?"

"Stay where you are. Don't move until you hear I'm off the airplane."

There were lights off to the left of the aircraft, and steps were being rolled over. The ramp was rolled back toward the center door, and LaBeet was ready to leave the cockpit. The mass murderer had a few parting words for the flight crew: "Sorry for the inconvenience. Have a Happy New Year."

No one moved. They remained in their seats, waiting, eyes straight ahead, unsure whether he had left the airplane. And then—and for some this was the most frightening moment of the trip—the cockpit door opened and there was a blinding flash of light. Korshin's reaction: "A bomb! It has to be a bomb! It's over! That's it!" A moment later they realized the blinding light came from the floodlights of a television camera crew poised just outside the cockpit.

And then the cockpit was suddenly crowded with Cuban officials telling them that it was all over. LaBeet was in custody.

A Mother in Mannville

by Marjorie Kinnan Rawlings

The orphanage is high in the Carolina mountains. Sometimes in winter the snowdrifts are so deep that the institution is cut off from the village below, from all the world.

I was there in the autumn. I wanted quiet, isolation, to do some troublesome writing. I was homesick, too, for the flaming of maples in October, and for corn and pumpkins and black-walnut trees and the lift of hills. I found them all, living in a cabin that belonged to the orphanage, half a mile beyond the orphanage farm. When I took the cabin, I asked for a boy or man to come and chop wood for the fireplace when it got cold.

I looked up from my typewriter one late afternoon, a little startled. A boy stood at the door, and my pointer dog was at his side and had not barked to warn me. The boy was probably twelve years old, but undersized.

He said, "I can chop some wood today."

"You? But you're small."

"Size don't matter, chopping wood," he said. "Some of the big boys don't chop good. I've been chopping wood at the orphanage a long time."

"Very well. There's the ax. Go ahead and see what you can do."

An hour and a half later, the boy said, "I have to go to supper now. I can come again tomorrow evening."

I said, "I'll pay you now for what you've done," thinking I should probably have to insist on an older boy.

"Ten cents an hour?"

"Anything is all right."

We went together back of the cabin. An astonishing amount of solid wood had been cut.

"But you've done as much as a man," I said. "This is a splendid pile."

I looked at him, actually, for the first time. His hair was the color of the corn, and his eyes, very direct, were like the mountain sky when rain is coming—gray, with a shadowing of that miraculous blue. I gave him a quarter.

"You may come tomorrow," I said, "and thank you very much."

He looked at me, and at the coin, and seemed to want to speak, but could not, and turned away.

At daylight I was half wakened by the sound of chopping. When I left my bed in the cool morning, the boy had come and gone, and a stack of wood was neat against the cabin wall. He came again after school in the afternoon and worked until time to return to the orphanage. His name was Jerry; he was twelve years old, and he had been at the orphanage since he was four. I could picture him at four, with the same grave gray-blue eyes and the same—independence? No, the word that comes to me is "integrity."

The word means something very special to me, and the quality for which I use it is a rare one. My father had it—there is another of whom I am almost sure—but almost no man of my acquaintance possesses it with the clarity, the purity, the simplicity of a mountain stream. But the boy Jerry had it. It is bedded on courage, but it is more than brave. It is honest, but it is more than honesty. The ax handle broke one day. Jerry said the woodshop at the orphanage would repair it. I brought money to pay for the job and he refused it.

"I'll pay for it," he said. "I broke it. I brought the ax down careless."

"But no one hits accurately every time," I told him. "The fault was in the wood of the handle. I'll see the man from whom I bought it."

It was only then that he would take the money.

And he did for me the unnecessary thing, the gracious thing, that we find done only by the great of heart. He found a cubbyhole beside the fireplace that I had not noticed. There, of his own accord, he put a little wood, so that I might always have dry fire material ready in case of sudden wet weather. I found that when I tried to return his thoughtfulness with such things as candy and apples, he was wordless. He only looked at the gift and at me, and a curtain lifted, so that I saw deep into the clear well of his eyes, and gratitude was there, and affection, soft over the firm granite of his character.

He made simple excuses to come and sit with me. I could no more have turned him away than if he had been physically hungry. I suggested once that the best time for us to visit was just before supper, when I left off my writing. After that, he waited always until my typewriter had been some time quiet.

He became intimate, of course, with my pointer, Pat. There is a strange connection between a boy and a dog. It is difficult to explain, but it exists. When I went across the state for a weekend, I left the dog in Jerry's charge. He was to come two or three times a day and let out the dog, and feed and exercise him. I should return Sunday night.

My return was belated, and fog filled the mountain passes so treacherously that I dared not drive at night. The fog held the next morning, and it was Monday noon before I reached the cabin. The dog had been fed and cared for that morning. Jerry came early in the afternoon, anxious.

"The superintendent said nobody would drive in the fog," he said. "I came just before bedtime last night and you hadn't come. So I brought Pat some of my breakfast this morning. I wouldn't have let anything happen to him."

"I was sure of that. I didn't worry."

"When I heard about the fog, I thought you'd know."

He was needed for work at the orphanage and he had to return at once. I gave him a dollar in payment, and he looked at it and went away. But that night he came in the darkness and knocked at the door.

"Come in, Jerry," I said, "if you're allowed to be away this late."

"I told maybe a story," he said. "I told them I thought you would want to see me."

"That's true," I assured him, and I saw his relief. "I want to hear about how you managed with the dog."

He sat by the fire with me and told me of their two days together. The dog lay close to him and found a comfort there. And it seemed to me that being with my dog, and caring for him, had brought the boy and me, too, together, so that he felt that he belonged to me as well as to the animal.

We watched the flames.

"That's an apple log," he said. "It burns the prettiest of any wood."

We were very close.

"You look a little bit like my mother," he said. "Especially in the dark, by the fire."

"But you were only four, Jerry, when you came here. You have remembered how she looked, all these years?"

"My mother lives in Mannville," he said.

For a moment, finding that he had a mother shocked me as greatly as anything in my life has ever done, and I did not know why it disturbed me. Then I understood my distress. I was filled with passionate resentment that any woman should go away and leave her son. A fresh anger added itself. A son like this one—I burned with questions I could not ask. In any, I was afraid, there would be pain.

"Have you seen her, Jerry—lately?"

"I see her every summer. She sends for me."

I wanted to cry out. "Why are you not with her? How can she let you go away again?"

He said, "She comes up here from Mannville whenever she can. She doesn't have a job right now."

His face shone in the firelight.

"She wanted to give me a puppy, but they can't let any one boy keep a puppy. You remember the suit I had on

last Sunday?” He was plainly proud. “She sent me that for Christmas. The Christmas before that”—he drew a long breath, savoring the memory—“she sent a pair of skates.”

“Roller skates?”

My mind was busy, making pictures of her, trying to understand her. She had not, then, entirely deserted or forgotten him. But why, then— I thought, “I must not condemn her without knowing.”

“I'm going to take the dollar you gave me for taking care of Pat,” he said, “and buy her a pair of gloves.”

I could only say, “That will be nice. Do you know her size?”

“I think it's eight and a half,” he said.

He looked at my hands.

“Do you wear eight and a half?”

"No. I wear a smaller size, a six."

"Oh! Then I guess her hands are bigger than yours."

I hated her. He was taking his dollar to buy gloves for her big stupid hands, and she lived away from him, in Mannville, and contented herself with sending him skates.

"She likes white gloves," he said. "Do you think I can get them for a dollar?"

"I think so," I said.

And after my first fury at her, we did not speak of her again. His having a mother of any sort at all, not far away, in Mannville, relieved me of the ache I had had about him. He was not lonely. It was none of my concern.

He came every day and cut my wood and did small helpful favors and stayed to talk. The days had become cold, and often I let him come inside the cabin. He would lie on the floor in front of the fire, with one arm across the pointer, and they would both doze and wait quietly for me.

I was ready to go.

I said to him, "You have been my good friend, Jerry. I shall often think of you and miss you. Pat will miss you too. I am leaving tomorrow."

He did not answer. When he went away, I remember that a new moon hung over the mountains, and I watched him go in silence up the hill. I expected him the next day, but he did not come. I stopped by the orphanage and left the cabin key and money for my light bill with Miss Clark.

"And will you call Jerry for me to say good-bye to him?"

"I don't know where he is," she said. "I'm afraid he's not well. He didn't eat his dinner this noon. One of the boys saw him going over the hill. He was supposed to fire the boiler this afternoon. It's not like him; he's unusually reliable."

I was almost relieved, for I knew I should never see him again, and it would be easier not to say good-bye to him.

I said, "I wanted to talk with you about his mother—why he's here—but I'm in more of a hurry than I expected to be. But here's some money I'd like to leave with you to buy things for him at Christmas and on his birthdays. It will be better than for me to try to send him things. I could so easily duplicate—skates, for instance."

"There's not much use for skates here," she said.

Her stupidity annoyed me.

"What I mean," I said, "is that I don't want to duplicate things his mother sends him. I might have chosen skates if I didn't know she had already given them to him."

She stared at me.

"I don't understand," she said. "He has no mother. He has no skates."

The Moonlit Road

by Ambrose Bierce

STATEMENT OF JOEL HETMAN, JR.

I am the most unfortunate of men. Rich, respected, educated, and of sound health, I sometimes think that I should be less unhappy if this good fortune had been denied me, for then the contrast between my outer and my inner life would not demand such painful attention.

I am the only child of Joel and Julia Hetman. My father was a well-to-do country gentleman, my mother a beautiful and accomplished woman to whom he was jealously and passionately devoted. The family home was a few miles from Nashville, Tennessee.

At the time of which I write, I was nineteen years old, a student at Yale. One day I received a telegram from my father of such urgency that I left at once for home. At the railway station in Nashville, a distant relative awaited me to explain the reason for my recall: My mother had been barbarously murdered—why and by whom none could guess, but the circumstances were these:

My father had gone to Nashville, intending to return the next afternoon. Apparently prevented from accomplishing his business, he returned the same night, arriving just before dawn. In his testimony before the police, he explained that since he had no latchkey and did not want to disturb the sleeping servants, he had gone round to the rear of the house. As he turned the corner of the building, he heard a sound as of a door gently closed. He saw in the darkness, indistinctly, the figure of a man, which instantly disappeared among the trees of the lawn. A hasty pursuit and brief search of the grounds proving fruitless, he entered at the unlocked door and mounted the stairs to my mother's chamber. The door was open. Stepping into black darkness, he fell headlong over some heavy object on the floor. It was my poor mother, dead of strangulation by human hands!

Nothing had been taken from the house, and the servants had heard no sound. Excepting those terrible finger-marks upon the dead woman's throat—dear God! that I might forget them!—no trace of the assassin was ever found.

I gave up my studies and remained with my father, who, naturally, was greatly changed. He had fallen into so deep a depression that nothing could hold his attention.

One night, a few months after the dreadful event, my father and I walked home from the city. The full moon was out, and the entire countryside had the solemn stillness of a summer night. Black shadows of bordering trees lay across the road, which gleamed a ghostly white. As we approached the gate to our dwelling, my father suddenly stopped and clutched my arm, saying, hardly above his breath: "God! God! What is that?"

"I hear nothing," I replied.

"But see—see!" he said, pointing along the road, directly ahead.

I said: "Nothing is there. Come, Father, let us go in—you are ill."

He had released my arm and was standing rigid and motionless in the center of the roadway, staring like one crazed with distress. I pulled gently at his sleeve, but he had forgotten my existence. Presently he began to move backward, step by step, never for an instant removing his eyes from what he saw, or thought he saw.

At that moment, my attention was drawn to a light that suddenly streamed from an upper window of the house. When I turned to look for my father, he was gone. In all the years that have passed since, I have never heard a whisper of his fate.

Statement of Caspar Grattan

Today I am said to live. Tomorrow, here in this room, will lie a senseless shape of clay that all too long was I.

Some, doubtless, will inquire, "Who was he?" In this writing, I supply the only answer that I am able to make—Caspar Grattan. Surely, that should be enough. The name has served my small need for more than twenty years of a life of unknown length. True, I gave it to myself, but lacking another, I had the right.

Standing upon the shore of eternity, I turn now for a last look landward over the course by which I came. There are twenty years of footprints fairly distinct, the impressions of bleeding feet. They lead through poverty and pain, wandering and unsure, as of one staggering beneath a burden.

Backward beyond the beginning of this suffering, I see nothing clearly; it comes out of a cloud. I know that it spans only twenty years, yet I am an old man.

I only know that my first consciousness was of maturity in body and mind. I found myself walking in a forest, weary and hungry. Seeing a farmhouse, I approached and asked for food, which was given to me by someone who asked my name. I did not know, yet knew that all had names. Greatly embarrassed, I retreated, and night coming on, lay down in the forest and slept.

The next day I entered a large town, which I shall not name. Nor shall I relate further incidents of the life that is now to end—a life of wandering, always and everywhere haunted by an overmastering sense of terror in punishment of crime.

It seems I once lived near a great city, a prosperous planter, married to a woman whom I loved and distrusted. We had one child.

One luckless evening it occurred to me to test my wife's faithfulness. I went to the city, telling her that I should be absent until the following afternoon. But I returned before daybreak and went to the rear of the house, purposing to enter by a door I had left unlocked. As I approached it, I heard it gently open and close, and saw a man steal away into the darkness. With murder in my heart, I sprang after him, but he had vanished. Sometimes now I cannot even persuade myself that it was a human being.

Crazed with jealousy and rage, I entered the house and sprang up the stairs to the door of my wife's chamber. It was closed, but I easily entered and, despite the darkness, soon stood by the side of her bed. My groping hands told me that it was empty.

"She is below," I thought, "and has evaded me in the darkness of the hall."

But as I was leaving, my foot struck her, huddled in a corner of the room. Instantly my hands were at her throat, stifling a shriek, my knees were upon her struggling body. There in the darkness, without a word of accusation or blame, I strangled her till she died!

There ends the dream. Again and again the tragedy repeats itself in my consciousness—over and over I lay the plan, I suffer the confirmation, I remedy the wrong.

There is another dream, another vision of the night. I stand among the shadows in a moonlit road. The trees sigh out a warning. I am aware of another presence. In the shadow of a great dwelling, I catch the gleam of white garments; then the figure of a woman confronts me—my murdered wife! There is death in the face; there are marks upon the throat. The eyes are fixed on mine with an infinite gravity. There is no blame in them, only recognition. Before this awful figure, I retreat in terror—a terror that is upon me as I write. I can no longer rightly shape the words. The incident ends where it began—in darkness and in doubt.

Yes, I am again in control of myself. After all, it is only a life-sentence. "To Hell for life"—that is a foolish penalty: the culprit chooses the duration of his punishment. Today my term comes to an end.

Statement of the Late Julia Hetman, Through the Medium Bayrolles

I had retired early and fallen almost immediately into a peaceful sleep, from which I awoke with a sense of peril. My husband, Joel Hetman, was away from home; the sevants slept in another part of the house. But these were familiar conditions; they had never before distressed me. Nevertheless, the strange terror grew so immense that I sat up and lit the lamp at my bedside. This gave me no relief; the light seemed rather an added danger, for I reflected that it would shine out under the door, disclosing my presence to whatever evil thing might lurk outside.

Extinguishing the lamp, I pulled the bedclothing about my head and lay trembling and silent.

At last it came—a soft, irregular sound of footfalls on the stairs! They were slow, hesitant, uncertain, as of something that did not see its way. To my disordered reason they were all the more terrifying for that, signaling the approach of some blind and mindless evil to which there is no appeal. We know this well, we who have passed into the Realm of Terror, who reside in eternal dusk among the scenes of our former lives, yearning for speech with our loved ones, yet dumb, and as fearful of them as they are of us. Sometimes the disability is removed, the law suspended: by the deathless power of love or hate we break the spell—we are seen by those whom we would warn, console, or punish.

Oh God! What a thing it is to be a ghost, fearful and shivering in an altered world, a prey to anxiety and despair!

No, I did not die of fright: the Thing turned and went away. I heard it go down the stairs, hurriedly. Then I rose to call for help. Hardly had my shaking hand found the doorknob when—merciful heaven!—I heard it returning. I fled to a corner and crouched upon the floor. I tried to pray. I tried to call the name of my dear husband. Then I hear the door thrown open. There was an interval of unconsciousness, and when I revived, I felt a strangling clutch upon my throat—felt my arms feebly beating against something that bore me backward—felt my tongue thrusting itself from between my teeth! And then I passed into this life.

No, I have no knowledge of what it was. Of this existence we know many things, but no new light falls upon any page of all that went before death. I lingered long near the dwelling where I had been so cruelly changed to what I am. Vainly I sought some method of presenting myself, some way to make my continued existence and my great love and deep pity understood by my husband and son.

One night I searched for them without success; they were nowhere in the house, nor about the moonlit lawn. I left the lawn and moved in the white light and silence along the road, aimless and sorrowing. Suddenly I heard the voice of my poor husband in exclamations of astonishment, with that of my son, who was trying to reassure him. There by the shadow of a group of trees they stood—near, so near! Their faces were toward me, the eyes of the elder man fixed upon mine. He saw me—at last, at last, he saw me! The death-spell was broken: Love had conquered Law! I moved forward, smiling and consciously beautiful, to offer myself to his arms, to comfort him with soft words.

Alas! His face went white with fear, his eyes were as those of a hunted animal. He backed away from me, as I advanced, and at last turned and fled into the wood—to what end it is not given to me to know.

To my poor boy left doubly desolate, I have never been able to impart a sense of my presence. Soon he, too, must pass to this Life Invisible and be lost to me forever.

Find the one correct answer.

Cause/Effect 1. ______ Mr. Carr asked Alfred to wait a moment before he left because
a. he wanted to confront Alfred about the things he had been stealing.
b. he liked Alfred and wanted to get to know him better.
c. he thought Alfred had been doing a good job and he wanted to give him a raise.
d. he knew Alfred's father worked evenings and wasn't home much, so he thought Alfred might like to have an older man he could talk with.

Substitutions 2. ______ Read the following sentence: "But Sam Carr only nodded his head a few times, and then Alfred grew very frightened and he didn't know what to say." The word *he* refers to
a. Sam Carr.
b. Alfred's father.
c. Alfred.
d. a local cop.

Scanning 3. ______ Alfred's father was a
a. drugstore owner.
b. printer.
c. cop.
d. thief.

Sequence 4. ______ Which of the following happened second?
a. Alfred got in trouble for the first time.
b. Sam Carr caught Alfred with things he had stolen in his pockets.

c. Sam Carr hired Alfred to work in his drugstore.
d. After talking with Alfred's mother, Mr. Carr fired Alfred, but he decided not to call the police about him.

Inference △ 5. ______ Why did Mr. Carr finally decide not to call the police about Alfred?
a. He was in trouble with the law himself, so he didn't want to deal with the police.
b. He was impressed by Alfred's mother and wanted to please her.
c. he realized that Alfred hadn't really stolen anything.
d. He had a boy about Alfred's age, so he had sympathy for Alfred.

Character/ Feelings 6. ______ How did Alfred feel about the way his mother had talked to Mr. Carr?
a. Angry
b. Sad
c. Frightened
d. Proud

Scanning 7. ______ How did Alfred and his mother get home from the drugstore?
a. They took a taxi.
b. They took a bus.
c. Alfred's father picked them up in his car.
d. They walked.

Character/ Feelings 8. ______ How did Alfred's mother feel as she poured herself a cup of tea?
a. Strong and self-assured
b. Frightened and trembling
c. Angry and upset
d. Peaceful and content

Tone 9. ______ The tone of this story is
a. serious.
b. humorous.
c. mysterious.
d. suspenseful.

Main Idea ○ 10. ______ This story is mainly about
a. a woman who doesn't know what to do about her son, who is always getting in trouble.
b. a drugstore owner who can't make up his mind whether or not to call the police about an employee he knows has been stealing from him for quite some time.
c. a boy whose mother comes to help him out when he gets in trouble at work and how he gains a new understanding about what her life is like.
d. what it's like to work in a drugstore in a big city.

Check your answers with the key.

IA-2 **ACCENT ON ABILITY**

Find the one correct answer.

Context Clues 1. ______ As it is used in this selection, the word *personnel* means
a. pertaining to a person.
b. personal.
c. pertaining to employees.
d. working for a large and successful company.

Scanning 2. ______ What was the name of the new organization that Hank Viscardi left his job as director of a personnel department to head?
a. Fordham School for the Disabled
b. Just One Break
c. The Human Resources and Training Institute
d. The Red Cross Service League

Inference △ 3. ______ Why did Hank Viscardi decide to take the new job?

a. His wife and friends told him that he should take the job.
b. He wanted to earn more money and have a more secure future.
c. He felt he hadn't yet fulfilled his obligation to the disabled.
d. He felt it would be a more meaningful thing for him to do with his life.

Problem/ Solution 4. ______ How did Hank Viscardi solve the problem of his stumps wearing out?

a. He spent the rest of his life in a wheelchair.
b. He took his friend's advice and went to be fitted with artificial legs.
c. He had an operation that restored the circulation in his stumps.
d. He decided not to work or go to school ever again, so that his stumps would be able to rest.

Scanning 5. ______ How old was Hank Viscardi when he reached the height of five feet, eight inches tall?

a. Eighteen
b. Twenty-one
c. Twenty-six
d. Thirty-seven

Substitutions 6. ______ Read the following sentence: "He was able to join the Red Cross, which planned to use him as a field officer—not as a hospital worker, as he had wished." The word *which* refers to

a. the Red Cross.
b. a hospital worker.
c. a field officer.
d. what he had wished.

Sequence

7. ______ Which of the following happened third?

a. Hank Viscardi served as a field officer for the Red Cross during World War II.
b. Hank Viscardi worked as head of the personnel department of a large and successful company.
c. Hank Viscardi agreed to head a new organization aimed at finding jobs for the disabled.
d. Hank Viscardi established the Human Resources Research and Training Institute.

Fact/
Opinion

8. ______ Which of the following statements from the selection is a fact?

a. They were married on November 16, 1946, and moved into a remodeled garage on Long Island, a garage belonging to Hank's old friend, Dr. Yanover.
b. Hank Viscardi was thirty-seven years old when he made the most important decision of his life.
c. His entire life, from the day he was born, had been a preparation for such work.
d. He felt he had been born again, and he was overcome with emotion.

Character/
Feelings

9. ______ What kind of person is Hank Viscardi?

a. Selfish and concerned only with material things
b. Fearful and easily discouraged
c. Strong, determined, and generous
d. Intelligent, but unable to accomplish anything

Main Idea ○ 10. ______ This selection is mainly about
a. how artificial limbs are constructed and how people learn to use them.
b. Hank Viscardi's successful life as head of the personnel department of a large and successful company.
c. how Hank Viscardi met and courted a woman who became his wife on November 16, 1946.
d. Hank Viscardi's life and the many ways he has used his abilities to serve others.

Check your answers with the key.

IA-3 ONE GOOD TIME

Find the one correct answer.

Substitutions 1. ______ Read the following sentence: "His gait was shuffling, his hair scanty and gray, and he had that expression of patience which comes from long waiting, both of body and of soul." The word *which* refers to
a shuffling.
b. hair that is scanty and gray.
c. that expression of patience.
d. long waiting.

Character/ Feelings 2. ______ What did William Crane feel toward Narcissa?
a. Anger
b. Hatred
c. Fear
d. Love

Sequence 3. ______ Which of the following happened third?
a. Narcissa agreed to marry William Crane and not to go away again.

b. Narcissa and her mother spent all the insurance money.
c. Narcissa's father died, and she and her mother received a large amount of money from his insurance company.
d. Narcissa and her mother went to New York.

Scanning

4. ______ How long were Narcissa and her mother gone on their trip to New York?
a. Three days
b. Six days
c. Six weeks
d. A year

Cause/Effect

5. ______ Why did Narcissa and her mother return to their hometown?
a They decided they would rather save some of the insurance money instead of spending it all at once.
b. They ran out of money.
c. William Crane wrote Narcissa a letter asking her to marry him, so she convinced her mother they should go back.
d. They broke the law in New York and were asked to leave at once.

Problem/Solution

6. ______ How did Narcissa and her mother pay for tickets home when they realized they were all out of money?
a. Narcissa asked William Crane to send them enough money for the trip home.
b. The railroad company decided to let them ride for free.
c. Narcissa did some needlework for a wealthy woman in New York and saved enough money to pay for the tickets.

d. Narcissa explained their situation to the people at the hotel in New York, and they gave them the tickets.

Scanning 7. ______ What did Narcissa give to William Crane when she got back from New York?
a. A wedding ring
b. A fur cape
c. A gold watch
d. A hat

Inference △ 8. ______ How would Richard Stone probably have felt about the way his daughter and wife spent the insurance money?
a. Shocked
b. Happy
c. Relieved
d. Proud

Character/Feelings 9. ______ What kind of person is William Crane?
a. Selfish
b. Loyal and understanding
c. Cruel
d. Proud and domineering

Main Idea ○ 10. ______ This story is mainly about
a. Richard Stone, a tyrant who was confined for many years to an armchair until his death finally freed his wife and daughter from his control.
b. Narcissa, a young woman who goes to New York with her mother and spends all their inheritance money in six days, then returns to her hometown to the man who had waited for her for years.

c. William Crane, a middle-aged man who has waited for years for the chance to marry Narcissa Stone, and who is heartbroken when she decides to go to New York instead of marrying him after her father dies.
d. the many ways to spend a lot of money quickly when you're on a trip to New York.

Check your answers with the key.

IA-4 THE BET

Find the one correct answer.

Cause/Effect

1. ______ What brought about the bet between the banker and the young lawyer?
   a. A discussion over which horse would win at the races
   b. An argument comparing capital punishment with life imprisonment
   c. A disagreement over whether people can survive when they are all alone
   d. An argument concerning money

Scanning

2. ______ How many years did the young lawyer have to remain imprisoned in order to win the bet?
   a. Five
   b. Ten
   c. Fifteen
   d. Twenty

Scanning

3. ______ Which of the following was the prisoner not allowed to do during his imprisonment?
   a. To read books
   b. To drink wine
   c. To write letters
   d. To receive letters

Inference △ ______ 4. Why did it take the prisoner a whole year to read the New Testament?

a. He was a very slow reader.
b. He spent most of his time playing the piano.
c. He was carefully studying all its teachings.
d. He knew he couldn't have any more new books for a while, so he wanted to make this one last.

Figurative Language 5. ______ Which of the following sentences from the story contains an example of personification?

a. He fell on these subjects so hungrily that the banker hardly had any time to get books enough for him.
b. A damp, penetrating wind howled in the garden and gave the trees no rest.
c. The color of his face was yellow, of an earthy shade; the cheeks were sunken, the back long and narrow, and the hand upon which he leaned his hairy head was so lean and skinny that it was painful to look upon.
d. In your books I cast myself into bottomless pits, worked miracles, burned cities to the ground, preached new religions, conquered whole countries.

Substitutions 6. ______ Read the following sentence: "Trying to make no sound, he took out of his safe the key of the door that had not been opened for fifteen years, put on his overcoat, and went out of the house." The word *that* refers to

a. his safe.
b. the key.
c. the door.
d. the house.

Sequence 7. ______ Which of the following happened second?

a. The prisoner began to study languages and history
b. The banker got the key to the door, entered the prisoner's chambers, and read the letter he had written.
c. At a party in autumn, the banker and one of his guests made a strange bet.
d. The banker locked the prisoner's letter in his safe.

Comparison 8. ______ The banker compares the prisoner's hair to that of a

a. skeleton.
b. shaggy dog.
c. gray horse.
d. woman.

Character/ Feelings 9. ______ How did the banker feel after he read the prisoner's letter?

a. Angry and ungrateful
b. Ashamed and relieved
c. Anxious and upset
d. Joyful and unburdened

Main Idea ○ 10. ______ This story is mainly about

a. what happens when two men make a bet about whether the younger one will be able to stand fifteen years of imprisonment.
b. the debate over whether life imprisonment is better or worse than capital punishment.
c. how a young lawyer got a lot of reading done over the course of fifteen years.
d. how a wealthy banker lost a lot of money over a foolish bet.

Check your answers with the key.

Find the one correct answer.

Figurative Language

1. ______ Which of the following sentences from the story contains a simile?
   a. But this evening is turning out to be a fine one—cool and foggy.
   b. It drops without a sound through the dead center of the bare iron rim.
   c. He is lifting his nose to the wind like a spaniel; he is gauging air currents.
   d. Officially, Coney Island is deemed to be a part of the endless rapidly changing scene that is New York City.

Scanning

2. ______ When did the city build housing projects in Coney Island?
   a. In the early 1960s
   b. In the late 1950s
   c. In the early 1980s
   d. In the late 1970s

Comparison

3. ______ Which of the following tells how Russell and Corey are not alike?
   a. Russell likes basketball while Corey does not.
   b. Russell is much younger than Corey.
   c. Russell is more serious and disciplined than Corey.
   d. Russell is much taller than Corey.

Character/ Feelings

4. ______ How did Russell feel after the fight with his girlfriend?
   a. Relieved c. Hopeless
   b. Furious d. Indifferent

Scanning 5. ______ How are Corey and Stephon related?

a. They are best friends.
b. They are cousins.
c. They are brothers.
d. They are uncle and nephew.

Substitutions 6. ______ Read the following sentence: "Corey is lulling defenders with his sleepy eyes, then exploding to the basket, where he casually tosses the ball through the hoop."

The word *where* refers to

a. the basket.
b. the hoop.
c. Coney Island.
d. the defenders.

Cause/Effect 7. ______ What is the effect of the Coney Island residents having little to be proud of?

a. They have lost all hope.
b. They have left the neighborhood.
c. They have let the toughs take over.
d. They have put all their hopes and pride in basketball.

Inference Δ8. ______ Why are Russell, Corey, and Stephon able to play so well?

a. They were taught the game by the top coaches in the Big East.
b. They have a natural ability which allows them to play well without much practice or effort.
c. Having few other opportunities to escape the ghetto, they have concentrated from a very young age on playing the game of basketball well.

d. The players they are competing against are not very good.

Sequence 9. _____ Which of the following happened second?

a. Stephon arrived at the court.
b. Chaos broke out on the court.
c. Russell started to warm up on the court.
d. Corey mimicked the TV announcer.

Main Idea ◯ 10. _____ This selection is mainly about

a. the importance of basketball to the residents of Coney Island.
b. how well Russell plays basketball.
c. how Coney Island is isolated from the heart of New York City.
d. the friendship of Russell, Corey, and Stephon.

Check your answers with the key.

IA-6 THE YOUNGEST MISS PIPER

Find the one correct answer.

Scanning 1. _____ What was Thomas Sparrell's job at the beginning of the story?

a. Clerk at the general store
b. Assistant to the judge
c. Senator
d. Geologist

Substitutions 2. _____ Read the following sentence: "There was a nasty scene between the youngest Miss Piper and the combined forces of her father and older sisters, which ended in Delaware's absolute refusal to attend the picnic at all if they intended to have it at Reservoir Canyon." The word *it* refers to

a. the combined forces of her father and older sisters.
b. the picnic.
c. Reservoir Canyon.
d. a nasty scene.

Scanning

3. ______ What did Delaware Piper do instead of attending the picnic?

a. She stayed at home and read a good book.
b. She went for a walk in the forest with Tom Sparrell.
c. She went down to the general store and had a talk with Tom Sparrell.
d. She chopped wood with the ax she had found.

Cause/ Effect

4. ______ What made the walls of the reservoir burst?

a. An earthquake
b. Thunder and lightning
c. A storm
d. An avalanche

Problem/ Solution

5. ______ How did Thomas Sparrell and Delaware Piper save the picnickers from the oncoming flood?

a. They convinced them not to hold the picnic at Reservoir Canyon.
b. They shouted down to them to climb up some nearby trees.
c. They redirected the oncoming water by quickly building a dam across the head of the trail.
d. They ran down to the general store and got someone to ride down into the valley and rescue them

Inference △ 6. ______ Why didn't Tom Sparrell and Delaware stay around to greet the picnickers they had rescued?

a. They were naturally shy and didn't know how to accept praise.
b. They had to return the ax to its owner, but first they wanted to make sure that no one else was in danger.
c. They wanted to go get married before Delaware's father could stop them.
d. They had done their good deed, but they didn't care to have anything more to do with the people who had refused to take their advice in the first place.

Character/Feelings 7. ______ What did Delaware Piper feel toward Tom Sparrell?

a. Gratitude and awe
b. Fear and hatred
c. Love and respect
d. Pity and concern

Figurative Language 8. ______ Which of the following sentences from the story contains a simile?

a. At first glance it seemed as if the trail was actually moving, wriggling its way down the mountain like a huge snake swollen to twice its usual size.
b. And it wasn't because of her slight deafness, which sometimes made us say things too loudly that we would rather have whispered behind closed doors.
c. When at last the appointed hour had arrived, the picnic party passed down the twisting mountain in a fever of enthusiasm.

d. He was interrupted by a faint crashing and crackling sound, and looking up saw a good-sized boulder bounding into the forest.

Sequence 9. ______ Which of the following happened third?

a. Delaware Piper warned the picnickers not to hold their picnic at Reservoir Canyon.
b. Delaware Piper announced that she was going to marry Tom Sparrell.
c. Tom Sparrell and Delaware Piper discussed geology at the general store.
d. Tom Sparrell, with Delaware Piper's help, rescued the picnickers from the oncoming flood.

Main Idea ○ 10. ______ This story is mainly about

a. the differences between the words "grocery" and "geology."
b. the worn-out walls of the Pioneer Ditch Company's huge reservoir, and how they had been rendered more dangerous by hasty repairs.
c. Delaware Piper's courtship with Tom Sparrell, and how the two rescue some picnickers from a flood.
d. Judge Piper's reasons for thinking that Tom Sparrell wasn't good enough for his daughter.

Check your answers with the key.

Find the one correct answer.

Inference △ 1. ______ Which of the following creatures would the author be most likely to distrust?
a. A pigeon
b. A wolf
c. A hornet
d. An octopus

Scanning 2. ______ How many eyes do most scorpions have?
a. Zero
b. Two
c. Eight
d. Twelve

Substitutions 3. ______ Read the following sentence: "Their blindness is so pronounced, evidently, that it has been a mystery how scorpions could ever find their way to a meal." The word *their* refers to
a. blindness.
b. a mystery.
c. scorpions.
d. humans.

Cause/Effect 4. ______ Which of the following is *not* listed in the selection as a possible effect of a scorpion sting?
a. Impaired vision
b. Irregular breathing
c. Subnormal temperature
d. Vomiting

Recognizing Bias/Author's Viewpoint 5. ______ Which of the following sets of words from the selection reveals the author's viewpoint concerning scorpions?
a. Beautiful, sleek, unadorned, binocular

b. Handsome, dangerous, group
c. Cluttered, useful, cover
d. Disgusting, nasty, uneasy

Scanning

6. ______ How did the bark scorpion get its name?
a. The only thing it eats is bark.
b. It has a habit of hiding behind loose and fallen pieces of tree bark.
c. Its back and legs look like little pieces of dark brown tree bark.
d. It makes a sound like a dog barking before it stings people.

Sequence

7. ______ Which of the following happened second?
a. Just before being stung by a scorpion, Doug Peacock decided to sit up late to read *Moby Dick* by the light of his campfire.
b. Doug Peacock sat down in a clearing and laid his hand back on a scorpion, which stung him.
c. Doug Peacock beat to death the scorpion that had just stung him.
d. Doug Peacock rolled over in his sleeping bag in the desert and was stung by a scorpion.

Figurative Language

8. ______ Which of the following sentences from the selection contains a simile?
a. They also carry a nasty stinger hanging overhead on the end of a long tail, like a sharpened spear ready to plunge.
b. Snakes are among my favorite living things—beautiful, sleek, unadorned, binocular.

c. Scorpions are more cluttered with useful hardware than a Swiss Army knife.
d. A scorpion drops from the roof of a house into a baby's crib, a young child runs barefoot through a garden, an adult carelessly picks up a piece of firewood, and whammo.

Fact/Opinion 9. ______ Which of the following statements from the selection is a fact?
a. Poison isn't the problem; a rattlesnake has poison, yet a rattlesnake is merely handsome and dangerous.
b. Another 69,000 Mexicans annually survive a sting that is at least bad enough to report.
c. My own heartfelt conviction is that scorpions are perhaps the most disgusting group of animals on the face of the earth, even including toy poodles.
d. Otherwise they would surely, like us, prefer to avoid the entire experience.

Main Idea ○ 10. ______ This selection is mainly about
a. what books to read when you're camping out in the desert.
b. why the author thinks snakes are beautiful even though they may be dangerous.
c. what to do if you are stung by a black widow spider and are far from a hospital.
d. scorpions and why the author particularly dislikes them.

Check your answers with the key.

Find the one correct answer.

Cause/Effect

1. ______ Why did Ben Crosby hire Velvet Pants?
   a. The Constable asked him to.
   b. He was looking for someone to teach his daughter how to play the guitar.
   c. He wanted to help Velvet Pants out, even though he didn't really need any more workers.
   d. He was short of hired hands and needed more workers.

Substitutions

2. ______ Read the following sentence: "Mrs. Crosby opened the door and saw a small man standing there; his face was a rich brown; his eyes were black and fearful; he appeared to be ready to flee if the occasion demanded it." The word *it* refers to
   a. the occasion.
   b. fleeing.
   c. the door.
   d. his face.

Scanning

3. ______ How did Velvet Pants greet Mrs. Crosby?
   a. With a bow
   b. With a handshake
   c. With a hug
   d. With a kiss

Character/Feelings

4. ______ How did Velvet Pants feel when he saw lightning bugs for the first time?
   a. Happy
   b. Angry
   c. Scared
   d. Sad

Figurative Language	5. _______	Which of the following sentences from the story contains a simile? a. The man comprehended, and his velvet-clad legs twinkled upstairs toward his bedroom. b. I remember how scared I was when I saw the first automobile come roaring and snorting along the road. c. I need hands worse than ducks need ponds. d. He's willing enough, but he handles a hayfork as dainty as if it was a toothpick.
Scanning	6. _______	Why didn't Velvet Pants dive in to save Johnny Nelson? a. He was a coward. b. He didn't like Johnny Nelson and didn't want to help him. c. He didn't know how to swim. d. He didn't realize that Johnny Nelson needed help.
Inference	△ 7. _______	Why did Johnny Nelson pretend to be drowning? a. Pete High put him up to it, so they could show everyone what a coward Velvet Pants was. b. He was hot and just wanted to have some fun cooling off. c. He liked Janey Crosby and thought her sympathies would be aroused if she saw him in danger. d. He was playing a practical joke on Pete High.
Character/ Feelings	8. _______	What did Pete High feel toward Velvet Pants? a. Sympathy c. Admiration b. Fear d. Contempt

Sequence 9. ______ Which of the following happened third?

a. Velvet Pants was forcibly seized and pressed into service aboard a ship.
b. Johnny Nelson pretended to be drowning, but Velvet Pants didn't dive in to save him.
c. Velvet Pants started giving guitar lessons to Janey Crosby.
d. Velvet Pants started working as one of Ben Crosby's farm hands.

Main Idea ○ 10. ______ This part of the story is mainly about

a. how Janey Crosby took guitar lessons from one of her father's farm hands, whom everyone called "Velvet Pants."
b. how Velvet Pants came to work for Ben Crosby and gained a reputation as a coward.
c. the time Johnny Nelson, the best swimmer in the county, almost drowned at the swimming hole.
d. the first time Velvet Pants ever saw lightning bugs.

Check your answers with the key.

• IA-9 THE UNFAMILIAR, PART 2

Find the one correct answer.

Inference △ 1. ______ Why did Janey Crosby decide to invite Velvet Pants to her birthday party?

a. She was inviting everyone, so of course she included him.
b. She felt sorry for him.
c. She was trying to get back at Pete High.
d. She wanted to hear him play his guitar.

Scanning

2. ______ Why did Velvet Pants sing Janey Crosby a song?
   a. He was in love with her and wanted her to marry him.
   b. He wanted to pick a fight with Pete High.
   c. He always liked to sing at parties.
   d. It was her birthday and he had no other gift to give her.

Scanning

3. ______ Why wouldn't Velvet Pants fight with Pete High?
   a. He was a coward.
   b. He didn't know how to fight.
   c. He had an appointment to keep and didn't have time for fighting.
   d. He didn't believe in violence.

Sequence

4. ______ Which of the following happened last?
   a. Velvet Pants rescued Janey Crosby from the bull.
   b. Pete High tried to start a fight with Velvet Pants, but he wouldn't fight back.
   c. Janey Crosby invited Velvet Pants to join her birthday party.
   d. Velvet Pants sang a song for Janey Crosby.

Figurative Language

5. ______ Which of the following sentences contains a metaphor?
   a. They brought presents as if they were bringing a tribute to a queen, and Janey, as graciously as a reigning sovereign, took them all and smiled.
   b. His owner, Ben Crosby, had raised him from a calf, wobbly on his legs, into a massive ton-and-a-half bull, with a chest like a haystack, a voice like

thunder, and the temper of a demon.

c. Velvet Pants was a tiger, completely sure of himself.

d. It was a small man in velvet trousers, and he was strolling toward Defender Monarch as casually and calmly as if the bull were a rosebush.

Substitutions 6. ______ Read the following sentence: "By blind luck Ben Crosby was able to trick him into entering a big pen, but in the process Defender Monarch had given a sample of his viciousness by ripping Johnny Nelson's arm from elbow to shoulder." The word *him* refers to

a. Ben Crosby.

b. Johnny Nelson.

c. Defender Monarch.

d. Velvet Pants.

Cause/ Effect 7. ______ What caused Janey Crosby to fall into the bull pen?

a. Someone pushed her.

b. The bull knocked her in.

c. The top rail gave way and she fell in.

d. She fainted and fell in.

Theme 8. ______ Which of the following best states the theme of this story?

a. It's natural to fear the unfamiliar and bravely face the known.

b. You can't judge a person by the clothes he or she wears.

c. It takes a crisis to bring out the best in everyone.

d. Action speaks louder than words.

Character/ Feelings — 9. ______ What did Ben Crosby feel toward Velvet Pants after the incident with the bull?

a. Anger
b. Disgust
c. Fear and pity
d. Amazement and gratitude

Main Idea ○ 10. ______ This part of the story is mainly about

a. why Velvet Pants was such a coward.
b. Janey Crosby's birthday party and what happened there.
c. how Crosby Corners learned that it had misjudged Velvet Pants.
d. Defender Monarch, a huge bull owned and raised by Ben Crosby.

Check your answers with the key.

IA-10 OTHER PEOPLE ARE HER BUSINESS

Find the one correct answer.

Context Clues — 1. ______ As it is used in this selection, the word *paraplegic* means

a. someone who has lived a long life.
b. a friend who knows what it's like to feel down.
c. someone whose legs are paralyzed.
d. someone in a wheelchair.

Scanning — 2. ______ What is Sharon McGrory-Buckley's job title?

a. Medical social worker
b. Head nurse
c. Associate director of social work
d. Patient advocate

Scanning

3. ______ Which of the following is *not* listed in the selection as being one of Buckley's roles?
   a. Psychological counselor
   b. Patient advocate
   c. Detective
   d. Religious adviser

Problem/ Solution

4. ______ How did Buckley help Mr. B solve the problem of where to live when he left the hospital?
   a. She helped him arrange for a 24-hour aide and other support so he could return to his own apartment.
   b. She talked with his daughter and convinced her to take her father in and care for him.
   c. She found a nursing home that allowed its residents a great deal of independence, which made Mr. B feel more comfortable with that option.
   d. She helped him regain his strength to the point where he would be safe and comfortable living by himself.

Substitutions

5. ______ Read the following sentence: "But the point is to keep him out of the hospital, and if we send him home alone in his condition, this man is likely to be back here before long." The word *here* refers to
   a. the man's home.
   b. the hospital.
   c. Buckley's office.
   d. Long Island.

Sequence

6. ______ Which of the following happened third?
   a. Stanley retired at the early age of 59 so he could fully enjoy his retirement years.

b. Buckley drew up an intensive recovery program for Stanley.
c. Stanley went for a medical examination and discovered he had a walnut-sized growth on his brain.
d. Stanley had a mild headache on the tennis court and found he couldn't hit the ball.

Fact/Opinion 7. ______ Which of the following statements from the selection is an opinion?
a. Armed with updated information, Buckley proceeds on her rounds, visiting each patient on her list—her average caseload is 15 to 20.
b. In the course of any day, her duties might involve everything from counseling a heart patient about surgery or preparing a cancer victim for death to phoning patients' relatives, arranging nursing home admissions, setting up home-care plans, or preparing insurance applications.
c. Nobody cares more about the people who need her, and nobody is better at bringing resources to bear.
d. She had melanoma, a form of skin cancer that can spread throughout the body.

Character/Feelings 8. ______ What kind of person is Sharon McGrory-Buckley?
a. Insensitive and self-pitying
b. Cold, uncaring, and lazy
c. Hard-working, but ineffective
d. Skillful, determined, and caring

Inference △ 9. ______ Why does Buckley feel it doesn't pay to project ahead about her patients' cases?

a. She realizes she has no way of predicting the future, so it's not worth trying.
b. She knows that many of her patients will get sicker, and it is more effective to concentrate on what she can do to help them in the present.
c. She doesn't care that much about her patients and so doesn't want to fill her mind with needless worrying about them.
d. She knows her patients will get angry at her if she tells them the truth about what will happen to them.

Main Idea ○ 10. ______ This selection is mainly about

a. a young woman who died of melanoma at the age of 23 while studying for her master's degree.
b. a run-in Sharon McGrory-Buckley had one day with a friend of hers who is a paraplegic.
c. Sharon McGrory-Buckley's job as a medical social worker.
d. what happened to Mr. B when he got out of the hospital.

Check your answers with the key.

IA-11 DESCENT INTO THE MAELSTROM

Find the one correct answer.

Figurative Language 1. ______ Which of the following sentences from the story contains an example of personification?

a. The interior, as far as the eye could fathom it, was a smooth, shining, and jet-black wall of water, speeding dizzily round and round.
b. The hurricane was a cruel master; at its first puff, both our masts went overboard.
c. The boat made a sharp half turn to the left, and then shot off in its new direction like a thunderbolt.
d. The boat appeared to be hanging, as if by magic, midway down, upon the interior surface of the vast and spiraling funnel.

Substitutions 2. ______ Read the following sentence: "We wanted to cross the channel at slack water, which is when the water is between tides and is neither flowing in nor flowing out." The word *which* refers to
a. slack water. c. flowing out.
b. flowing in. d. the channel.

Cause/Effect 3. ______ What caused the death of the guide's younger brother?
a. He was swept into the maelstrom and drowned.
b. The hurricane swept the mast he was tied to overboard.
c. The ring-bolt he was holding on to broke.
d. He fell from the top of one of the boat's masts and was killed.

Character/Feelings 4. ______ What did the guide feel when his brother tried to force his hands from the ring-bolt?
a. Rage
b. Despair
c. Grief
d. Relief

Problem/ Solution	5. ______	How did the guide manage to survive being swept into the center of the maelstrom? a. He clung to the ring-bolt for all he was worth and waited for the whirlpool to quiet down. b. He let go of the ring-bolt and swam back up to the surface of the ocean. c. He held on to the barrel and stayed with the boat until it rose to the surface again. d. He noticed that cylindrical objects descended more slowly, so he cut the barrel loose from the boat and stayed with it until it rose to the surface.
Sequence	6. ______	Which of the following happened third? a. The guide's boat plunged into the center of the maelstrom. b. A hurricane struck the guide's boat. c. The guide's boat was pulled into the outer rim of a maelstrom. d. The guide was rescued by a passing boat.
Scanning	7. ______	Why didn't the guide's old mates recognize him? a. He had been gone such a long time, and they had short memories. b. His clothes were soaking wet, and he was a complete mess. c. His appearance had been changed by the ordeal he had gone through. d. They had been blinded during the storm and couldn't see him clearly.

Figurative Language 8. ______ Which of the following sentences from the story contains a simile?

a. It was slack tide, but the sea still heaved in mountainous waves from the effects of the hurricane.
b. The boat made a sharp half turn to the left, and then shot off in its new direction like a thunderbolt.
c. The hurricane was a cruel master; at its first puff, both our masts went overboard.
d. How often we made the circuit of the belt it is difficult to say.

Inference △ 9. ______ What made the guide's hair turn white?

a. Old age
b. The swirling water of the maelstrom
c. Fear
d. Relief

Main Idea ○ 10. ______ This story is mainly about

a. the narrator's feelings about the guide who told him a frightening story.
b. an experience the guide had of narrowly escaping alive after going into the center of a maelstrom.
c. why sailors fear hurricanes so much.
d. the guide's relationships with his two brothers, both of whom died at sea following a hurricane.

Check your answers with the key.

IA-12 EXPLORING THE AMAZON

Find the one correct answer.

Scanning 1. ______ What was Paula DiPerna doing for Jacques Cousteau's Amazon expedition?

a. Camera work
b. Consulting
c. Flying a helicopter
d. Advance work

Scanning 2. ______ Where is the source of the Amazon River?
a. In the Atlantic Ocean
b. In New York
c. In Manaus, a city in the middle of the Amazon jungle in Brazil
d. In the Andes

Context Clues 3. ______ As it is used in this selection, the word *tributary* means
a. a river or stream that feeds into a larger river or stream.
b. both above and below water.
c. exploring the deep forest.
d. the intricate beauty of the largest rain forest on earth.

Substitutions 4. ______ Read the following sentence: "I since have calculated that in the course of my Amazon stay I placed some 4000 phone calls, about half of which did not go through on the first attempt." The word *which* refers to
a. the course of DiPerna's Amazon stay.
b. the first attempt.
c. the phone calls.
d. DiPerna's calculations.

Sequence 5. ______ Which of the following happened third?
a. DiPerna flew to Brasilia to meet with the Cousteaus.
b. DiPerna arrived for the first time in Manaus.
c. DiPerna watched the fishermen free some dolphins that had accidentally gotten trapped in their nets.

d. DiPerna spent the afternoon with some miners she later learned were murderers who cut the air hoses of other miners.

Figurative Language

6. ______ Which of the following sentences from the selection contains a simile?

a. Little light penetrates, but a rainstorm can make the most densely packed trees shudder.
b. The taxi sounded as though it once had been a washing machine.
c. The Rio Negro is only one of the thousand great and small rivers that lace the forest and can rise a dozen feet with the rainy season and then fall away drastically.
d. The rain forest itself is a beautiful, tangled green web of trees, trees, trees, as far as the eye can take it in from plane or from land.

Comparison

7. ______ The author compares the feel of the dolphins' skin to

a. the last light of day.
b. warm ice melting.
c. a triumphant circle.
d. a sleek jet.

Character/ Feelings

8. ______ Looking back from the perspective of New York, how does DiPerna feel about her months on the Amazon?

a. Basically good
b. Sorry she wasted her time
c. Relieved to be away from the sound of rain pounding like a thousand nails being hammered
d. Basically bad

Inference △ 9. ______ Which of the following does the author probably miss the least from her time on the Amazon?

a. Mosquitos
b. Dolphins
c. Fishermen
d. Birds

Main Idea ○ 10. ______ This selection is mainly about

a. how Jacques Cousteau's boat, the *Calypso*, was built.
b. the contrast between Paula DiPerna's life in New York and her life during eleven months on the Amazon.
c. Paula DiPerna's adventures and impressions while doing advance work on the Amazon for one of Jacques Cousteau's expeditions.
d. Paula DiPerna's close call with some miners who murder other miners they don't like by cutting their air hoses while they are diving.

Check your answers with the key.

IA-13 THE CALIFORNIAN'S TALE

Find the one correct answer.

Scanning 1. ______ What was the narrator doing before he met Henry?

a. Mountain climbing
b. Gardening
c. Prospecting
d. Camping

Substitutions 2. ______ Read the following sentence: "It had the look of being lived in and petted and cared for and looked after; and so had its front yard, which was a garden of flowers, abundant and flourishing." The word *which* refers to

a. a garden.
b. flowers.
c. it.
d. its front yard.

Character/ Feelings	3. ______	What kind of person was Henry's wife? a. Kind and thoughtful b. Angry and hostile c. Nasty and domineering d. Disorganized and untidy
Cause/ Effect	4. ______	Why did the narrator decide to stay with Henry through the weekend? a. He had no place better to go. b. He thought he might find some gold in the stream down the road from Henry's house. c. He wanted to meet Henry's friends. d. He wanted to meet Henry's wife.
Character/ Feelings	5. ______	What did Henry's friends feel toward him? a. Anger b. Pity and love c. Gratitude d. Envy and disgust
Sequence	6. ______	Which of the following happened third? a. Henry's wife went away for a brief stay with her people. b. Henry's friends explained to the narrator that they had drugged Henry so he could get to sleep. c. The narrator arrived at Henry's house and was invited to stay until Sunday so he could meet Henry's wife. d. Henry's wife disappeared.
Figurative Language	7. ______	Which of the following sentences from the story contains an example of personification? a. Their instruments danced with the eager anticipation of the lady's return.

b. Nothing here that hasn't felt the touch of her hand.
c. He had hardly swallowed his drink when the clock began to strike.
d. There, now tell her to her face you could have stayed to see her, and you wouldn't.

Scanning 8. ______ What happened to Henry's wife?
a. She decided to extend her visit to her people by a few weeks.
b. She arrived after Henry fell asleep.
c. She took sick and died nineteen years earlier.
d. She was captured by Indians and never heard from again.

Inference △ 9. ______ Why did Henry's friends act as if his wife were still alive?
a. They were playing a joke on him.
b. They cared about him and thought it would be easier for him if they went along with his belief that his wife was still alive.
c. They were also insane and thought that Henry's wife really was still alive.
d. They wanted an excuse to have a party.

Main Idea ○ 10. ______ This story is mainly about
a. a prospector who strikes it rich in the hills of California.
b. a young woman of nineteen who has gone for two weeks to visit her people, who live forty or fifty miles away.
c. how the narrator came to meet the charming wife of a man named Henry.

d. the narrator's visit with a man named Henry, who is awaiting the return of his wife, even though she really died many years earlier.

Check your answers with the key.

IA-14 ALWAYS RUNNING

Find the one correct answer.

Scanning

1. _____ Who is Mr. Rothro?
   a. A friend of Mr. Rodríguez
   b. The principal of Taft High School
   c. The former principal of Luis's elementary school
   d. Luis's former counselor at Continuation High School

Substitution

2. _____ Read the following sentence: "In fact, I believe you're probably doing better than most young people—even better, I'm afraid, than some who *are* going to school." The word *some* refers to
   a. school.
   b. doing better.
   c. probably.
   d. young people.

Character/ Feelings

3. _____ How does Luis feel about his father's job?
   a. Enthusiastic and happy
   b. Ashamed and disappointed
   c. Frightened
   d. Indifferent

Fact/ Opinion

4. _____ Which of the following statements from this selection is an opinion?
   a. "I think you'll find our industrial arts subjects more suited to your needs."
   b. My father worked in the biology labs and maintained the science department's museum and weather station.

c. The first day of school, a Taft High School counselor called me into her office.
d. The classes she enrolled me in were print shop, auto shop and weight training.

Cause/Effect 5. ______ At first what causes Luis to spend so much time in the library?
a. He loves to read all kinds of books.
b. He waits for his father to finish his work.
c. He meets his friends there.
d. He likes the librarian.

Comparison 6. ______ What similarity do the books on the special shelf share that makes them so meaningful for Luis?
a. They are books about minority experiences to which Luis can relate.
b. They are all written by Mexican-Americans like Luis.
c. They are all about the area in which Luis lives.
d. They are all books suggested by Luis's English teacher.

Character/Feelings 7. ______ What motivates Luis to storm out of his English class?
a. He is in a hurry to see his father.
b. Another student makes fun of him.
c. He believes the assigned book to be insulting to Mexicans.
d. The teacher won't allow him to read the book of his choice.

Scanning 8. ______ What gift does Luis say his father gave him?
a. A good education
b. Words of encouragement
c. The world of books
d. Loving guidance

Inference Δ 9. ______ With which of the following statements would Luis Rodríguez be most likely to agree?
a. You should play it safe and not try new things.

b. Schools should be more sensitive to the individual needs of their students.
c. Only read books that relate to your specific experience.
d. Many times it doesn't pay to stand up for what you believe.

Main Idea ◯ 10. _____ This selection is mainly about
a. how Luis Rodríguez's wrote his book.
b. Luis Rodríguez's experiences while attending Taft High School and his discovery of the joy of reading.
c. Mr. Rodríguez's job as a janitor and how it affected his relationship with his son.
d. Mrs. Rodríguez's attempts to get her son to go back to school.

Check your answers with the key.

IA-15 THE JEWELS OF M. LANTIN

Find the one correct answer.

Comparison 1. _____ The narrator compares the beauty of M. Lantin's wife to that of
a. a diamond necklace.
b. her rhinestone earrings.
c. an angel.
d. a superb wine.

Scanning 2. _____ Where did M. Lantin's wife like to go in the evenings?
a. To visit her mother
b. To the theater
c. To visit her women friends
d. Out to dinner with her husband

Character/ Feelings

3. ______ What did M. Lantin feel when his wife died?

a. Anxiety
b. Joy
c. Relief
d. Grief

Cause/ Effect

4. ______ Why did M. Lantin decide to sell his wife's necklace?

a. He wanted to forget her, and he couldn't bear to have her things around to remind him of her.
b. He was out of money and thought he could get six or seven francs for the necklace.
c. A jeweler called him up and asked him if he wanted to sell it.
d. His wife's mother advised him to sell it.

Inference

△ 5. ______ Why did M. Lantin ask the first jeweler if he was sure about the value of his wife's necklace?

a. He didn't trust the jeweler and thought he was trying to cheat him.
b. He was hard of hearing and hadn't understood what the jeweler said.
c. He had thought the necklace was artificial and couldn't believe it was worth so much.
d. His friends at work had told him that he should always ask this question because then the jeweler would be sure to offer more money.

Sequence

6. ______ Which of the following happened third?

a. M. Lantin's wife took sick after an evening out at the opera, and she died soon thereafter.

b. M. Lantin remarried.
c. M. Lantin discovered that his wife's jewelry was worth almost 200,000 francs.
d. M. Lantin took one of his wife's necklaces to a jeweler.

Figurative Language

7. ______ Which of the following sentences from the story contains a metaphor?
a. The smile that constantly graced her lips seemed a reflection of her heart.
b. When you haven't the means to wear real jewelry, you should show yourself adorned only with your own grace and beauty; these are the true pearls.
c. One wintry evening, when she had been at the opera, she came home shivering with cold.
d. He felt the earth shiver; a tree just before him seemed to crush him.

Scanning

8. ______ What did M. Lantin do immediately after receiving the money for all of his wife's jewels?
a. He went to an elegant restaurant to eat.
b. He remarried.
c. He took a cab and rode around.
d. He handed in his resignation at the office.

Substitutions

9. ______ Read the following sentence: "He went around shaking hands with his co-workers and telling them all about his plans for the future." The word *them* refers to
a. his co-workers.
b. his plans.
c. hands.
d. the jewelers.

Main Idea ○ 10. ______ This story is mainly about

a. a lovely young wife who likes to go to the theater wearing her artificial jewelry.
b. a man who discovers that his dead wife's jewelry, which he had thought was artificial, is worth almost 200,000 francs.
c. M. Lantin's job as chief clerk of the Minister of the Interior.
d. why M. Lantin decides to marry a young woman, even though she is only the daughter of a tax collector.

Check your answers with the key.

IA-16 A START IN LIFE, PART 1

Find the one correct answer.

Scanning 1. ______ Why was Daisy going to the country with Elmer Kruse?

a. She was going to start working for his family.
b. She was going to visit her Uncle Fred.
c. She was going to visit Elmer Kruse's wife.
d. She had never been to the country before, so her mother decided to send her on a drive with Elmer Kruse.

Scanning 2. ______ What did Mrs. Switzer do for a living?

a. She stayed at home and was a housewife.
b. She washed and cleaned for other people.
c. She worked in a dress shop mending clothes.
d. She babysat for other people's children.

Character/ Feelings	3. ______	How did Goldie and Dwight feel about their older sister? a. They hated her. b. They feared her. c. They looked up to her and envied her. d. They didn't care about her one way or the other.
Cause/ Effect	4. ______	Why didn't Mrs. Switzer manage to get Daisy's things all mended and "fixed up" before she went to the country? a. She hadn't realized that Elmer Kruse would be coming to get Daisy so soon. b. She didn't really care about Daisy, and so didn't want to go to the bother. c. She was so busy working for other people that she didn't have enough time. d. Her sewing machine was broken, and she didn't have any money to get it repaired in time.
Substitutions	5. ______	Read the following sentence: "She jammed what she could into the bag, thinking that it would have to do somehow." The word *it* refers to a. the things she could jam into the bag. b. the bag. c. thinking. d. Daisy's trip to the country.
Sensory Images	6. ______	Which of the following words from the story appeals to the sense of touch? a. Smoky c. Shout b. Black d. Clammy

Character/ Feelings

7. ______ How did Daisy feel as she drove in the car with Elmer Kruse through the country?

a. Excited
b. Angry
c. Depressed
d. Anxious

Sequence

8. ______ Which of the following happened second?

a. Daisy waved good-bye to her mother, sister, and brother.
b. Elmer Kruse returned to pick Daisy up.
c. Daisy's mother quickly helped her pack her bag.
d. Daisy and Elmer arrived at the Kruses' house.

Inference

△ 9. ______ Why was Mrs. Switzer troubled about the kind of life Daisy would have at the Kruses?

a. She knew the Kruses were mean people and would be unkind to Daisy.
b. Mrs. Switzer was the kind of woman who worried about everything.
c. She was worried because she hadn't had time to get Daisy "fixed up" before she left.
d. She knew from her own experience how difficult it was to work for other people.

Main Idea

○ 10. ______ This part of the story is mainly about

a. Elmer Kruse and the errands he had to do in town on the day he picked Daisy up.
b. Mrs. Switzer and her housekeeping duties.
c. how Daisy got ready to leave home and go to work for the Kruses in the country.

d. Daisy's brother and sister and why they looked up to her.

Check your answers with the key.

IA-17 A START IN LIFE, PART 2

Find the one correct answer.

Context Clues

1. ______ As it is used in this story, the word *valise* means
   a. whatever it is.
   b. a bag or suitcase.
   c. something used.
   d. a broken strap.

Scanning

2. ______ What reason did Daisy give the Kruses for not feeling well?
   a. She said she had a stomachache.
   b. She told them she was homesick.
   c. She said she had a toothache.
   d. She said she had the flu.

Sensory Images

3. ______ Which of the following phrases from the story appeals to the sense of sight?
   a. Raised her eyebrows
   b. Queer low ache
   c. Honked the horn
   d. A tremendous howl

Inference

△ 4. ______ Why did Edna Kruse make faces at her husband behind Daisy's back?
   a. She was feeling sick to her stomach and didn't want Daisy to know.
   b. She was a mean person and was making fun of Daisy.
   c. She wasn't satisfied with the job Daisy was doing.
   d. She wanted to make her husband laugh.

Cause/ Effect	5. ______	What made Billy start to cry when he and Daisy were alone in the kitchen? a. Daisy hit him. b. Daisy yelled at him because he wouldn't sit at the kitchen table. c. He missed his mother. d. Daisy wasn't letting him play with the blocks.
Substitutions	6. ______	Read the following sentence: "Mama and Goldie cared about her—but Daisy was away out in the country, and they were at home." The word *her* refers to a. Daisy. c. Goldie. b. Mama. d. Edna Kruse.
Sequence	7. ______	Which of the following happened third? a. Elmer gave Billy some lemon drops he had gotten for him in town. b. Edna Kruse sent Daisy off to help Billy play with his blocks. c. Daisy went off to her room to unpack her bag. d. The Kruses went off in their car and left Daisy alone in the house.
Character/ Feelings	8. ______	How did Daisy feel when the family went off on a visit and left her alone in the house? a. Relieved b. Happy and calm c. Angry d. Hurt and lonely
Tone	9. ______	The tone of this story is a. playful. c. serious. b. mysterious. d. joyful.

Main Idea ○ 10. ______ This part of the story is mainly about

a. Daisy's experiences and feelings when she starts working for the Kruses.
b. the proper way to care for young children.
c. the Kruses and the family outing they took one afternoon.
d. Daisy's toothache and why her mother hadn't taken her to a dentist when she first had it.

Check your answers with the key.

IA-18 SKYJACKED

Find the one correct answer.

Character/Feelings 1. ______ How did pilot Ken Korshin feel when he heard Jean say the prisoner had a gun to her head?

a. Amused
b. Outraged
c. Anxious
d. Afraid

Substitutions 2. ______ Read the following sentence: "The pilot knew there was a prisoner aboard—was he the one holding the gun or was one of the guards holding a gun on him?" The word *he* refers to

a. the prisoner.
b. one of the guards.
c. the pilot.
d. a flight attendant.

Scanning 3. ______ Why was Ishmael Ali LaBeet a prisoner?

a. He had demonstrated against the oppression of blacks.
b. He had killed a friend after a fight at a party.
c. He had murdered eight people as an act of protest.
d. He had violated a traffic law.

Scanning

4. ______ Where did LaBeet demand that the skyjacked jet take him?
a. Florida
b. The Virgin Islands
c. New York
d. Cuba

Inference

△ 5. ______ Why did LaBeet question the pilot's claim that there might not be enough fuel to reach their destination?
a. He was naturally suspicious and never trusted anybody.
b. He knew that this was a common claim made when planes were hijacked to discourage the hijacker.
c. He knew the pilot was a liar and could not be trusted to say anything truthful.
d. He was just joking around with the pilot—in fact, he believed what the pilot was telling him.

Setting

6. ______ The setting of this selection is
a. a jet hijacked off its course on Christmas Eve.
b. an airport in St. Croix on Christmas Eve.
c. a jet hijacked off its course on New Year's Eve.
d. an airport in St. Croix on New Year's Eve.

Recognizing Bias/ Author's Viewpoint

7. ______ Which of the following sets of words reveals the author's viewpoint toward LaBeet?
a. Revolutionary, butchered, mass murderer
b. Incident, scenery, instructions
c. Reason, permission, seat belts
d. Fuel, far-fetched, air controllers

Cause/Effect 8. ______ What caused the blinding flash of light that scared the pilot and crew?

a. A bomb thrown into the jet as LaBeet left
b. The floodlights of a television camera crew poised just outside the cockpit
c. A sudden storm with lightning and thunder
d. A police officer's flashlight

Fact/Opinion 9. ______ Which of the following statements from the selection is a fact?

a. Sorry for the inconvenience.
b. They would, then, land in Havana with 10,000 pounds of fuel, enough for an additional 50 minutes of flight.
c. Mr. Ali, we're a little short of fuel, and I really don't feel we have enough to make Havana.
d. The final half-mile seemed to take an hour instead of just a few seconds.

Main Idea ○ 10. ______ This selection is mainly about

a. the political situation in the Virgin Islands.
b. New Year's Eve celebrations in New York City.
c. a jet hijacked by Ishmael Ali LaBeet.
d. why pilot Ken Korshin decided to fill in on a flight when it was supposed to be his day off.

Check your answers with the key.

IA-19 A MOTHER IN MANNVILLE

Find the one correct answer.

Scanning 1. ______ What did the author do for a living?

a. She was a writer.

b. She was a teacher.
c. She raised dogs.
d. She ran an orphanage.

Character/ Feelings

2. ______ What did the author feel toward Jerry?
a. Anger and impatience
b. Fear
c. Love and respect
d. Indifference

Context Clues

3. ______ As it is used in this selection, the word *integrity* means
a. independence.
b. a quality of courage, honesty, and purity.
c. a word that means something very special and rare.
d. having the simplicity of a mountain stream.

Figurative Language

4. ______ Which of the following sentences from the selection contains a simile?
a. He only looked at the gift and at me, and a curtain lifted, so that I saw deep into the clear well of his eyes, and gratitude was there, and affection, soft over the firm granite of his character.
b. I could no more have turned him away than if he had been physically hungry.
c. His hair was the color of the corn, and his eyes, very direct, were like the mountain sky when rain is coming—gray, with a shadowing of that miraculous blue.
d. My return was belated, and fog filled the mountain passes so treacherously that I dared not drive at night.

Substitutions 5. ______ Read the following sentence: "The dog lay close to him and found a comfort there." The word *there* refers to
a. the author's house.
b. the orphanage.
c. the woodpile.
d. close to him.

Character/ Feelings 6. ______ What did the author feel toward Jerry's mother?
a. Passionate resentment
b. Pity
c. Love and admiration
d. Respect

Sequence 7. ______ Which of the following happened second?
a. Jerry told the author that his mother lived in Mannville.
b. A young boy, Jerry, showed up to chop the author's wood.
c. The author rented a cabin owned by an orphanage in the Carolina mountains.
d. The author asked Jerry to take care of her dog while she was away.

Inference △ 8. ______ Why did Jerry tell the author she looked like his mother?
a. He was a liar and wanted to make her feel bad.
b. He really thought the author did look a lot like his mother.
c. He felt close to the author and wanted her to know how much he liked her.
d. He was trying to trick her into giving him presents like the ones his mother gave him.

Scanning 9. ______ Why was the author going to leave money for Miss Clark to buy Jerry gifts instead of sending them to him herself?

a. She had a busy life and knew she wouldn't have time to get anything for him.
b. She was a forgetful person and was afraid she'd miss the important holidays.
c. She didn't know what kinds of things Jerry would like to have.
d. She didn't want to duplicate gifts his mother might give him.

Main Idea ○ 10. ______ This selection is mainly about

a. the author's relationship with a boy named Jerry during her stay at a cabin near the orphanage where he lived.
b. Jerry's mother and what her life in Mannville was like.
c. the special relationship that can grow between a boy and a dog, particularly if the boy is lonely.
d. the need for wood when it starts to get cold in the Carolina mountains.

Check your answers with the key.

IA-20 THE MOONLIT ROAD

Find the one correct answer.

Scanning 1. ______ How did Joel Hetman Jr.'s mother die?

a. She died of fright.
b. She had a heart attack.
c. She fell down the stairs and hit her head.
d. She was strangled to death.

Character/ Feelings	2. ______	What kind of man was Joel Hetman Sr.? a. Even-tempered and forgiving b. Jealous, possessive, and capable of violence c. Good-natured, easy-going, and kind d. Cold and distant
Sequence	3. ______	Which of the following happened third? a. Joel Hetman Sr. disappeared. b. Joel Hetman Jr. was summoned home because his mother had met a sudden death. c. Julia Hetman heard strange noises out on the stairs. d. Caspar Grattan found himself walking in a forest, weary and hungry.
Inference	△ 4. ______	Who was Caspar Grattan? a. Julia Hetman's secret lover b. Julia Hetman's son c. Julia Hetman's husband d. A crazy man completely unrelated to the Hetmans
Inference	△ 5. ______	What did Caspar Grattan intend to do when he finished making the statement? a. Return to his former life b. Go to bed c. Change his name d. Kill himself
Character/ Feelings	6. ______	After she died, what did Julia Hetman feel toward her husband? a. A desire for vengeance b. Loving pity c. Fear d. Hatred

Figurative Language

7. ______ Which of the following sentences from the story contains an example of personification?

a. The trees sigh out a warning.
b. They lead through poverty and pain, as of one staggering beneath a burden.
c. His face went white with fear, his eyes were as those of a hunted animal.
d. In the shadow of a great dwelling, I catch the gleam of white garments; then the figure of a woman confronts me—my murdered wife!

Cause/Effect

8. ______ What was the cause of Joel Hetman Sr.'s disappearance?

a. He was afraid the police would find out that he had murdered his wife, so he decided to go into hiding.
b. He was murdered by Caspar Grattan, his wife's secret lover.
c. He fell over a tree root and was killed instantly.
d. He saw a vision of his murdered wife and fled in guilty terror.

Tone

9. ______ What is the tone of this story?

a. Humorous
b. Mysterious and sad
c. Light-hearted
d. Scholarly and instructive

Main Idea

○ 10. ______ This story is mainly about

a. how Caspar Grattan got his name.
b. Julia Hetman's life after death.
c. the murder of Julia Hetman and what followed it, told from the point of view of her son, her husband, and herself.

d. a respected, educated young man of sound health who wishes that the contrast between his outer and inner life were not so extreme.

Check your answers with the key.

ANSWER KEY

IA-1	IA-2	IA-3	IA-4	IA-5
1. a	1. c	1. c	1. b	1. c
2. c	2. b	2. d	2. c	2. a
3. b	△ 3. d	3. b	3. d	3. c
4. c	4. b	4. b	△ 4. c	4. c
△ 5. b	5. c	5. b	5. b	5. b
6. d	6. a	6. d	6. c	6. a
7. d	7. c	7. c	7. a	7. d
8. b	8. a	△ 8. a	8. d	△ 8. c
9. a	9. c	9. b	9. b	9. d
○ 10. c	○ 10. d	○ 10. b	○ 10. a	○ 10. a

IA-6	IA-7	IA-8	IA-9	IA-10
1. a	△ 1. d	1. d	△ 1. b	1. c
2. b	2. c	2. b	2. d	2. a
3. b	3. c	3. a	3. b	3. d
4. a	4. c	4. c	4. a	4. a
5. c	5. d	5. d	5. c	5. b
△ 6. d	6. b	6. c	6. c	6. c
7. c	7. a	△ 7. a	7. c	7. c
8. a	8. a	8. d	8. a	8. d
9. d	9. b	9. c	9. d	△ 9. b
○ 10. c	○ 10. d	○ 10. b	○ 10. c	○ 10. c

IA-11	IA-12	IA-13	IA-14	IA-15
1. b	1. d	1. c	1. c	1. c
2. a	2. d	2. d	2. d	2. b
3. b	3. a	3. a	3. b	3. d
4. c	4. c	4. d	4. a	4. b
5. d	5. d	5. b	5. b	△ 5. c
6. a	6. b	6. c	6. a	6. c
7. c	7. b	7. a	7. d	7. b
8. b	8. a	8. d	8. c	8. a
△ 9. c	△ 9. a	△ 9. b	△ 9. b	9. a
○ 10. b	○ 10. c	○ 10. d	○ 10. b	○ 10. b

IA-16	IA-17	IA-18	IA-19	IA-20
1. a	1. b	1. d	1. a	1. d
2. b	2. c	2. a	2. c	2. b
3. c	3. a	3. c	3. b	3. a
4. c	△ 4. c	4. d	4. c	△ 4. c
5. a	5. d	△ 5. b	5. d	△ 5. d
6. d	6. a	6. c	6. a	6. b
7. a	7. b	7. a	7. b	7. a
8. b	8. d	8. b	△ 8. c	8. d
△ 9. d	9. c	9. b	9. d	9. b
○ 10. c	○ 10. a	○ 10. c	○ 10. a	○ 10. c